M000158389

Finally Free

Breaking the Bonds of Depression Without Drugs

By Patty Mason

Finally Free: Breaking the Bonds of Depression Without Drugs

Copyright © 2011 by Patty Mason

ISBN 978-0-9829718-2-6

Printed by Liberty in Christ Ministries, Inc.
This book is available on-line through distributors worldwide.
To order: www.LibertyinChrist.net

Unless otherwise indicated, Bible quotations are taken from the HOLY
BIBLE, NEW INTERNATIONAL VERSION® Copyright © 1973, 1978,
1984 International Bible Society. Used by permission of Zondervan. All
rights reserved.

To request permission, please send your request to:
Patty@LibertyinChrist.net

Dedication

This book is dedicated to Angie,
and all those who are suffering,
or who have suffered, with depression.
There is always hope.

Table of Content

Preface

Before We Begin...

I want you to know you are not alone; "An estimated 33 to 35 million American adults are likely to experience depression at some point during their lifetime."[i] It is a crushing illness that pays no attention to age, nationality, gender, social status, or the color of one's skin. "Women especially are at risk; 30% of women are depressed, yet, 41% are too embarrassed to seek help."[ii] Yet, in spite of these overwhelming statistics, there is hope.

Right now, you may not feel hopeful. I know how you feel, because when I was deep in the pit of depression, I couldn't see any way out. I believed the darkness would never end. I know the pain you face every day. I know you are hurting emotionally, spiritually and physically. I know the sense of hopelessness and despair. I understand the isolation and the feelings of abandonment by others, even by those you once called friend. I know, more than anything, you long to end the madness and stop feeling like a prisoner in your own skin. I know, without a doubt, you ache to escape the emotional turmoil that is consuming and destroying your life. Yet, I also know, in the midst of my nightmare, I found freedom, even when I thought I never would. I found a way out of that well; and, now that I am on the other side of depression, I am here to tell you there is hope, there is an answer. There is a way to be *finally free!*

Throughout this book, I share my personal battle with depression, the struggles I faced, and the depth of despair that drove me to thoughts of suicide. Yet, through my story, I desire, more than anything, to offer hope to those suffering with depression.

Many things can cause depression, such as hormonal imbalance or a chemical inconsistency in the brain. Depression can also be caused by a life-altering event, such as the loss of a loved one, a tragic accident, loss of employment or financial debt. There are many life-altering incidents, circumstances and events that come along, and most of us, in our human nature, have a hard time effectively dealing with these situations. Even repressed emotions, such as anger or bitterness, can cause depression. Harboring unhealthy emotions, allowing them to fester and take root in the heart, can cause depression.

Depression comes in many forms; yet, no matter how or why depression comes into our lives, most of us, in a desperate attempt to get better, will turn to medication to find relief—I know I did. Yet, even though I sought pills, I never went on medication. Medication wasn't the answer to my problems.

I am not advocating drugs as a way to find release from depression, nor am I telling you not to take medication or seek medical advice—that is a personal decision. Depending on your condition and situation, medical treatment may be a good option for you. But medication was not what helped me to get out of my well of depression—and that's the story I want to share with you—how I became *Finally Free: Breaking the Bonds of Depression Without Drugs*.

As you read my story, my hope is that you will discover renewed strength, courage and determination—that you will find hope and freedom from your emotional hurt. Let my experiences inspire you to let go of a painful past, to move forward, and get to the root of your depression. Permit my story to bring you comfort in the midst of your suffering.

Thank you for giving me this opportunity to share my story with you.

With love,

Patty

1

The Trouble with Depression

I Never Saw it Coming

To know me today you would probably never guess I battled with depression; a prisoner who lived within the dark walls of torment, enslaved by despair and the fury of pent-up rage. You would probably never guess I lived through a darkness so blinding, a pain so unbearable, and an isolation so devastating, I became suicidal.

What is it about depression that brings a seemingly normal, sane woman to the brink of wanting to take her own life? What is it about depression that drives a soul to want to forsake her own existence and see death as an option for escape?

Perhaps for those who have never experienced depression, this may be an inconceivable concept—an unthinkable deduction of logic that is simply unreasonable. You may even become frustrated and wonder why people don't just get over depression. At least that's what my husband thought. It wasn't that he didn't care. At the time, he just didn't understand why I couldn't shake it off—to make the *choice* to be happy. But depression is not some temporary mood you wake up from and get over. People who have never experienced depression simply do not understand the difficult struggle we face every day.

Depression was a constant battle bringing on overwhelming feelings of sadness, anger, even rage, and hopelessness. I felt alone and lost—nothing mattered anymore. Feelings of guilt and worthlessness plagued my mind. I became restless, easily flustered and had trouble concentrating. I was in a miserable frame of mind and it didn't take long for me to begin having thoughts of death and suicide.

Depression, in my opinion, was far more than a disease or some type of mental illness; and it did far more than simply hurt. Depression was devastating, debilitating,

> Depression was a constant battle bringing on overwhelming feelings of sadness, anger, even rage, and hopelessness.

destructive and demoralizing. It crippled my mind, heart, spirit and soul and destroyed every part of me. Nothing kept me held in a world of pain and suffering like depression. It captured my soul and refused to let go. It was an unceasing vacuum gripping my soul in such a way that it rendered me utterly helpless and hopeless. I couldn't control what was happening. My once energetic personality lost its drive. I felt drained and tired, and I lost all interest to do anything or go anywhere.

When the depression hit, I became confused and wondered why this was happening to me. *Where did I go wrong?* At the time, I was seemingly living a good life, a life that appeared to be full of hopes and dreams, plans and expectations that kept me hungering for more. So what happened? How could the highest point of my life so quickly become the lowest point? It made no sense, but when the depression hit, my world came crashing down around me, and I didn't have the faintest idea how to begin to pick up the pieces, much less put my broken life back together.

I never saw the depression coming, nor did I realize how much it would steal from me. Nonetheless, depression hit my life like a freight train going about 90 miles an hour. I didn't expect it or plan for it; yet, there it was, like an unwelcomed guest in my home. Depression attached itself to my life and filled my days with gloom and misery.

The truth of the matter is no one ever sees depression coming into his/her life. They do not forecast it, nor plan for it. Depression is not a lifelong ambition. No one asks for it, desires it, deserves it, or relishes in the fact he/she has it. No one ever sets out to be depressed. It's a condition that forms without warning, like a dark storm that appears on the horizon of a sunny day, and suddenly destroys everything in its path.

My Story Begins...

Every story has a beginning. My story begins at the age of 18. Starting at this point may imply that I am jumping ahead, fast-forwarding to a convenience point and intentionally leaving out key moments in life that have played a distinctive role. But my story doesn't begin on the day I was born and work its way through a series of events that happened throughout life. My battle with depression unknowingly began on the day I decided to find myself.

The depression didn't surface at the age of 18, though. Actually, it appeared years later, when I was 35 to be exact. But depression has a root, and in order to fully appreciate my story and what I've been through, you need to know the origin and how it brought me to a point of despair. No depression story begins when the symptoms become visible. Mine began when I went down the paths I thought would bring me a sense of worth and fulfillment.

What I am sharing may seem odd at first. After all, why would a quest for fulfillment bring me, or anyone for that matter, to depths of despair when there are many other things that can bring any one of us to that point? For instance, depression can be brought on by hormonal imbalance or a chemical inconsistency in the brain. It can also be caused by a life-altering event, such as the loss of a loved one; a tragic accident, loss of employment or financial debt. For me, the depression could have taken root during my childhood or teen years.

Childhood, in my eyes, was not easy. I suffered a great deal of physical and emotional abuse. My father didn't understand love, and took a very militant and corporal approach to discipline. He didn't know any other way to rear his children, so he passed along the only method of discipline he knew and understood. As a result, I grew up terrified of my dad. My mother, on the other hand, was the exact opposite. She overcompensated for my father's form of strict physical discipline by offering no discipline at all. It was two extremes attempting to find a middle ground, both convinced their way of doing things was correct.

School was no refuge either. Among the other kids I was the outcast, the brunt of everyone's cruel jokes, and a constant source of teasing and harassment. I recall one recess in particular, when I was in the sixth grade, where a group of kids, both boys and girls, taunted me until they trapped me in a corner up against a brick wall. Once they realized I couldn't escape, they began to heave snowballs filled with rocks at my head and face. This went on until the school bell rang calling us back to class. No one saw, no one stopped the attack, and no one asked any questions. It was a mortifying incident I'll never forget.

> Like a dam breaking, the raging river burst through my broken heart, and wiped out anyone or anything in its path.

My family moved a great deal when I was young, and each time we moved I knew what was coming. Although I hoped it would be different, a chance to start over and leave the former things behind. Regrettably, it was always the same—the kids were the same, the mean jokes were the same, life in general was the same. Over time, the fear and humiliation grew to resentment, anger, and bitterness, adding to my already existing feelings of insecurity and loneliness.

The consequences of my suppressed emotions surfaced for the first time when I turned thirteen, and for years I lashed out at everyone around me, even those I loved. In what seemed like a flash, I went from being a sweet, shy, soft-spoken child to an angry teenager full of resentment. I began screaming at my family and throwing temper tantrums. I was very sensitive, so my feelings were easily hurt, which I released through fits of fury. I could no longer contain all those years of fear, hurt and abuse. Like a dam breaking, the raging river burst through my broken heart, and wiped out anyone or anything in its path.

All of these emotions took root in my heart and needed to be dealt with. But, at the age of 18, I didn't realize the effects my youth and childhood had on my soul, and I wouldn't until years later. At that time, all I could think about was moving on. My depression may have started then and lay dormant for years; like a masked thief stalking his prey, waiting for just the right time to pounce upon the unsuspecting victim. Perhaps the depression was caused by a cascade of events, a mixture of anger, fear and resentment; a concerto of disappointments, dashed dreams, and misguided expectations—a lifetime of events that finally took their toll. Whatever the reasoning, at the age of 18, I didn't see any of it. I didn't see depression, nor did I recognize the emotional problems that had taken root in my heart.

At 18, I was headed in a new direction, and all too happy to change course. I was done with my abusive childhood and turbulent teen years, or so I thought. At 18, I saw

> I was very sensitive, so my feelings were easily hurt, which I released through fits of fury.

nothing but promise and possibilities. I was ready for more than what I had experienced to date. I was determined to find what was missing. In those days I had a plan, or at least some idea of how I thought my life would turn out and the person whom I would become. I wanted much, and generally I had some idea of how I would accomplish it all. I craved success and an exciting career that would make me feel accomplished and talented. Somehow success represented a notch on the belt of life that told the world I had worth.

Along with that successful job, I desired to travel and see the world. I didn't want to grow old gracefully. No way, not me, I had plans. It was not only unthinkable to live an ordinary life, it was unacceptable. There was a great big world out there, and I wanted to embrace it all, or at least a large part of it. I wanted to sky-dive, climb mountains, and take every form of transportation known to man. I wanted to be the type of woman who rode a motorcycle at the age of fifty and had lots of wonderful adventure stories to tell her grandchildren.

This, of course, leads me to the most important aspiration of all—a family of my own. I wanted to find a husband —the man of my dreams—a man who would make me feel whole, as if somehow half of me was missing. Basically, I wanted that special person who would make me feel cherished and loved. Of course, I wanted children too. In my mind, I felt that giving birth to children would be my ultimate and greatest achievement. When in reality it gave me stretch-marks and sleepless nights. Don't get me wrong, I'm glad I had my children. I love them dearly, but I put a tremendous burden on them the day I thought they would somehow complete me as a person.

Plans, dreams, goals and having a vision for life are a good thing—even vital. Having dreams and aspirations can make us feel alive. The problem started, however, when I allowed those ambitions to define me. That's when I got into trouble. Somehow I thought I was going to be a better person, more successful and complete because I would have certain things, successes, and people in my life. Instead, I set myself up for a shattering blow of disappointment.

> Being a better person isn't about possessing things, money or a successful career. Yet, at the time, I didn't see it that way.

Being a better person isn't about possessing things, money or a successful career. Yet, at the time, I didn't see it that way. I was convinced that being emotionally and spiritually whole was found in success, marriage and children. I was persuaded that finding fulfillment was wrapped up in the quest I was about to take. This was the journey of a lifetime, and I had high expectations. I believed, without a doubt, I would find everything my soul longed for and craved.

2

Searching in All the Wrong Places

Empty Dreams—Empty Promises

The actual voyage began in my early twenties when I left my job at a successful bank in order to become a travel agent. It was a surprise to the people around me to make such a decision, but it gave me a lot more opportunity to travel. I took my first cruise when I was twenty-three, and from that time on, I was a world class traveler in search of an adventure that would make me feel alive. Over the course of the next five years, no grass grew under my feet. I took every plane, train, boat/ship and car ride I could, convinced that this sense of exploration was the best gift I could ever give myself.

A big part of me was restless, discontent with life, and who I was as a person. Looking back now, I believe what I was really doing was still trying to escape my past—maybe I was even trying to escape from myself. I must admit, though, when I was in some of those exotic places, I did feel like another person, someone who was living out her dreams and fulfilling her expectations. Over the years I took four cruises and traveled to Hawaii, Europe, Mexico, and several places across the United States. I had opportunities to go to the South Pacific, Hong Kong, Australia and South America. I loved it...while I was there. The trouble was, once my exciting escapade was over, I felt a deep sense of disappointment. As soon as I returned home, a sense of dissatisfaction would set in—a letdown that caused me to quickly strive for the next opportunity to travel. As a result, I quickly started pursuing the next trip, desperate for the next "adventure high." Travel became a drug—I couldn't get enough.

In my fifth year of travel exploration, I began to realize that this lifestyle wasn't working. Suddenly, I grew tired of airports and living out of a suitcase; yet, I still wanted more. It was like I was missing something; a void was growing in my soul, and I just didn't know how to fill it. Not one exotic place or exciting adventure gave me what I truly longed for. But, I was young and convinced there was still time to fill the longings of my soul. So, I began to think maybe it was time to find a man, settle down and then all my other dreams would surely come true.

Searching for Love

What is it about love, or the idea of being in love, that turns the head and heart of every girl? As a teenager I remember thinking about boys; and, even at the age of 14, I had some idea of the type of man I wanted to marry. It's funny how, as young ladies, we can develop an image of what we think "Mr. Right" will look and act like. For me, "Mr. Right" had to have a sense of humor. I loved to laugh, and I wanted a guy who could make me laugh, even if I felt down. I didn't want a clown, someone who was a silly goof; rather, I wanted a sincere, tender-hearted comedian who would help me look at the lighter side of life. I needed someone who was down-to-earth and easy-going, because I wasn't.

Even as a teenager I was a hard-working perfectionist, one who got the job done, and I carried that attitude into adulthood. I was that Type-A personality who felt that if the job had to be done right, I had to do it myself. Basically, in this area, I needed the opposite of me in order to balance my overzealous ways. I wanted someone who was generous, kind, considerate, and loving—a true gentleman. I didn't expect him to be perfect, just perfect

> What is it about love, or the idea of being in love, that turns the head and heart of every girl?

for me. As the years went by, my idea of "Mr. Right" dwindled, and I began to wonder if I would ever find what I was looking for.

As a teenager, finding that male companion had been very important. I remember searching early and yearning for that special connection—the one I believed would last forever. Unfortunately, when all the girls my age were dating, finding fun and new romance, I was experiencing a new awareness of loneliness and rejection. I assumed that if I didn't find a guy soon I was lost, doomed to wander the earth a hopeless romantic.

By the age of sixteen, I couldn't find anyone special. I had adopted the mindset that unless I had a boyfriend, I was incomplete. Without a guy part of me was missing—the better half—and without him I didn't have the foggiest idea how to replace it. I was cursed with the idea of finding a husband.

By the time I was 20, the rejection of high school had passed and I suddenly had men lining up at the door. What happened? What was different? How did I go from total loser to Miss America? The truth of the matter was, I was the same person I was at fourteen, sixteen, even eighteen, I had just developed a prettier face. My once overly skinny body took on some shape, my buck teeth had been fixed with braces, and my acne finally cleared up.

Now the race was on, and I needed to make up for lost time. I felt I had missed out on a lot of what other girls had already found, and I felt the need to catch up—fast. From age 20 until 28, I dated many men—some were short-term, others had longevity. Some I liked—others I didn't. I found dating fun and adventurous; yet, annoying and frustrating all at the same time. One of the biggest problems to dating was the connection with each of these men, or the lack thereof. If I liked him, he didn't like me, or if he liked me, I didn't like him. It was an unrelenting cycle, often met with disappointment and aggravation.

Sometimes I dated more than one man at a time. None of those relationships were serious, but I felt this approach was necessary, since I had such a late start at the dating game. During my all-out man hunt, I didn't sleep around. Somehow I held onto a strong sense of virtue that I wanted to keep. Even though I wanted to find that special man, I wasn't willing to have sex to get him. Intimate love was special, something to be cherished. As a woman, I had a lot to give and I felt that, in many ways, I had already given a great deal of whom I was as a person. Intimate love went deep, and it was something I didn't want to give away to just anyone. It was important enough, special enough, to be shared with that one person I loved enough to walk to the altar with. Then, and only then, would it be something special.

As a woman, I had a lot to give and I felt that, in many ways, I had already given a great deal of whom I was as a person.

Two men, in particular, made an indelible impression on my heart. Some relationships not only stick with us, they change us. The trouble was, even though I loved both of them (at different times); neither of them loved me back. I poured everything I had into those relationships. Yet, they offered nothing of value in return. At times, it made me feel like something was wrong with me—like somehow I wasn't good enough. Unfortunately, instead of moving on, the rejection only made me try harder. I wanted them to see what they were giving up; that I was the best thing that was ever going to happen to them. I didn't want to let either relationship go. No matter what, I was determined to make it work.

The trouble was, the harder I tried, the farther they ran. Both of these guys knew how I felt about them; yet, despite my open heart, they felt their love would be better spent elsewhere. It took me a long time to get over both of them.

Over the course of these eight years, there were many ups and downs. The high points were fun; even exhilarating. The times of disappointment and heartache felt life-shattering; and, at the time, I didn't think I would survive. But, in spite of all the good and bad, I longed to be married. I longed to take my place in society as a woman of honor, joined to my one true love. Instead, I kept coming up empty. With my weary soul still longing, I continued to face the world lost and utterly alone, worried I was destined to walk the earth forsaken.

Searching for Fulfillment

One day life changed when I finally married a man who I knew was deeply in love with me. He wasn't the man I dreamed of, but he was tender and would do anything in his power to try and make me happy. He was intelligent, engaging, and had a way of making me laugh. Our marriage was, and still is, a good one. We have been together, to this date, 23 years, and I couldn't picture myself with anyone else. Yet, somehow, as good of a husband and father as he is, he is not my all-in-all. Actually, no man should be.

It's almost amusing, or maybe it isn't, the way society sets a woman up to believe that she needs a man in order to be fulfilled. She is trained, from early childhood, to believe her single most important role in life is to be a wife and mother. When she doesn't accomplish that goal, she is somehow marked as rejected, undesirable, and unacceptable.

When I first married my husband, I had that mindset. I was looking for something or someone to fill the deep void in my soul. So, when a gentle-spirited man offered me the opportunity to find what I was looking for, I took it. He made me feel valued and special. He was like a warm blanket on a cold night, comfortable and inviting; a place of relaxation after a long, hard day. He was the ticket to finding everything I longed for, or so I thought.

At first, our marriage was sweet. We seemed to do well together. We were two very different people, and still are. He is an introvert, and I am an extrovert. He is a thinker, focusing on the intellectual stimulus of the circumstance, continually looking for a way to fix things, while, I, on the other hand, allow my emotions to run on high. To be honest, I often pour way too much passion into whatever situation I find myself in.

> It's almost amusing, or maybe it isn't, the way society sets a woman up to believe that she needs a man in order to be fulfilled.

Thinking back, I realize I gave up a large part of who I was as a person when I started dating my husband. I tried very hard to love the things that he loved, so I put the things I liked on the shelf. I loved to dance—he had two left feet. I loved roller coasters and adventure—he liked to stay home and watch TV. (By the way, to this day I still haven't gotten him on a roller coaster.) I liked romance and love stories—he made fun of them. He loved golf—I had never held a golf club. He liked chess—I didn't understand the game. His idea of a good time was ordering pizza and watching a movie on HBO—I was more apt to enjoy the night life. Somehow, through all of our differences, we made it work. I took up golf. I learned to play chess. And the night life went to sleep; all in exchange for what I thought would be something I truly wanted.

At first I enjoyed my new interests. It was fun letting him teach me; but it didn't take long for me to wonder where my own identity had gone. My name, my life, my interests and desires had suddenly become his name, his life, his interests and desires—I had somehow vanished. Instead of finding myself fulfilled in a meaningful, committed relationship—I got lost. Even though I felt we had a good marriage, my husband wasn't able to complete me the way I thought he should.

Searching for Happiness

Since neither a life of adventure nor marriage was giving me what I longed for, I tried fulfilling myself with a new adventure—children. Motherhood, could anything be better? Surely children would fill the void in my heart and give me the sense of happiness I was desperate to find. I knew from an early age I would one day be a mother. In fact, I wanted to have six children. I believed rearing children would be fun, a virtual playground of exciting moments filled with laughter and good times. I had no idea what I was getting myself into.

My husband and I talked about having children before we got married. So, for us, it was a natural course of action. However, since I was closing in on the age of 30, I was in a hurry to have children. If I was to have those six children, I had better get started—now. My biological clock was ticking, and soon became a loud drum in my hungry soul. I began to worry that if we didn't start right away, we wouldn't be able to have all of the children we wanted.

We weren't married a year when I became pregnant for the first time. Looking back, this became one of my biggest regrets —having children too soon after our marriage began. I simply wish I had given us a little more time to be a couple before we dove into the extended family

> Motherhood, could anything be better? Surely children would fill the void in my heart and give me the sense of happiness I was desperate to find.

plan. Over the next ten years, I became pregnant four times, and we were blessed with three beautiful healthy children: two girls and a boy. And then on March 12, 1999, our fourth child died while still in the womb.

The miscarriage was very difficult. I was well into the pregnancy and wearing maternity clothes. So, when I lost the baby, people around me noticed. Somehow kind and encouraging people didn't know how to act around me. I can't say that I blame them. What do you say when one week one of the mothers at your daughter's ballet class is obviously pregnant, and the next week she isn't?

For the first couple of days afterward, I felt like I was walking through a thick, blinding fog. Suddenly, I was an actor playing a part on stage and nothing was real. To some degree, this feeling of detachment helped me cope, at first. But, by the third day, hormones took over, and I began to have crying spells. A tidal wave of thoughts and emotions overtook my soul as I began to grasp the depth of our loss. The heartrending days that followed were extremely hard, and at times, I didn't think I would pull through. Then, about a week later, I received a phone call from the hospital informing me of the autopsy results. Apparently, our daughter's spinal cord wasn't attached to her brain, so even if she had lived, she would have been completely unable to do anything.

> I unknowingly placed an unfair burden on my children by expecting them to fulfill me as a person.

This news was hard, and I still missed her terribly. But, now I was able to release her, able to accept the hope that she was in a much better place.

Many years have come and gone since that time, and, as a family, we've been through a great deal. My children are big now; my oldest is in her twenties. For the most part, I enjoyed my children, and still do. But, like everything else in my life, I thought my children would somehow fill the emptiness in my heart—they didn't. I unknowingly placed an unfair burden on my children by expecting them to fulfill me as a person. I had assigned them an impossible task. They could never shape me into the person I was meant to be.

It didn't take long to realize motherhood wasn't going make me happy, or fill the needs and longings within my soul. So if motherhood couldn't make me happy, then what would? If I couldn't find meaning and purpose in life through adventure, a man, or children, then where could I go to find it?

Searching for Success

In the world's eyes there is something distinctive about carrying a banner of a successful career. It brings prestige, honor, and recognition that cannot be found anywhere else. The perks of such an honor include titles, accolades, rewards, and, of course, the added bonus of money. A high-ranking, successful career can be a launching pad to many great things in life; and, somehow, it denotes those who accomplish this high level of achievement as a man or woman of greatness.

When most people look at someone who is successful, they are filled with awe and respect; placing this person as one of exceptional importance. Who wouldn't want such a privilege, to be held in high esteem by those around him/her?

What pressure I put on myself, and allowed the world to put on me, when I believed I would have to achieve this level of prestige. In those days, I thought that reaching and striving after these things would make me happy, satisfied and content. It would somehow place me in a well-deserved category that would give me a level of accomplishment those around me would not only appreciate, but value. I wanted to be somebody, to make my mark on the world. I wanted to find a sense of purpose. Basically, I wanted to matter.

Before my so-called "successful" career days, when my days were filled with the daily responsibilities of marriage and motherhood, I would often encounter career women who would inevitably ask me the question: "So, what do you do?" I always dreaded this question, because every time I gave the normal response, "I'm a wife and mother," I felt looked down upon. Even though I had worked in the business world for eleven years prior to marriage, and was pursuing higher education, abruptly, and without warning, I went from someone of interest to someone insignificant. Within seconds of my "housewife" declaration, I found myself an outsider, an outcast among the professional women in the room.

When this happened I became disappointed, even disillusioned about my role as a young mother. Suddenly, I didn't measure up, and it made me feel less of a woman. At that time I didn't have a clear understanding or value of my purpose in the extraordinary role of motherhood. So, as the days and months went by, I became disheartened and bored; I even convinced myself that what I was doing wasn't anything worthwhile.

A growing sadness developed within me that made me feel lost in the mundane routine of wiping noses, watching Barney[iii] for the millionth time, and preparing yet another peanut butter and jelly sandwich. Somewhere between changing diapers and the endless loads of laundry, I lost the sense of who I was again and began to wonder what happened to that energetic young woman, who, at one time, was full of hopes and dreams.

Now that I am an older mother, and long past the disappointment and disillusionment that told me my children would somehow complete me, I see more clearly. Yes, my children are a mark on this world, they are a part of me, and I am a reflection of them, but they are not my all-in-all. Over the years, I have come to realize that being a mother is the hardest and most demanding job I could ever have.

Looking back, I am amazed, maybe even a little ashamed, to have allowed those other women to determine my worth based on what they thought success was. Being a mother is the most important job I've ever had. No other career, job, or project I've taken on has been able to equal it, or can compare to

> I wanted to be somebody, to make my mark on the world. I wanted to find a sense of purpose. Basically, I wanted to matter.

its high level of dedication and commitment. I'm just sorry it took me a long time to learn that lesson.

Over the years, I worked many jobs, and, for the most part did well at everything I put my hands on. I did earn that college degree, and I earned it with honors. I even accomplished this task while renovating a hundred-year-old Victorian home with my husband, and giving birth to our two daughters. I was seven months pregnant with our son the day I received my diploma. I recall the day vividly; the graduation gowns were silver, so I looked like a torpedo walking down the aisle.

In the working world, both before and after marriage, I won awards, was quickly given promotions and placed in positions of leadership. I was recognized before multitudes and was even named the number one sales consultant in the nation in my national area. I earned a car, received admiration from my colleagues, and was accepted into many well-respected organizations with open arms. In the world's eyes I had become a success. Unfortunately, the more success I found, the more miserable I became. It didn't make any sense. This wasn't how it was supposed to be. Where was my sense of accomplishment and purpose? Why was I still feeling empty, frustrated and discouraged? Why couldn't I find myself, and my reason for living?

3

Where Did I Go Wrong?

Hiding the Hurt, Masking the Pain

By the time I turned thirty-five, I had everything this world deems valid. I had a husband who loved me, three beautiful healthy children, a nice home, and a successful career. At this point, I was experiencing success at every phase of life, and I worked hard at convincing myself that I was leading a good life. My schedule was full of activities, programs and projects—I was burning the candle at both ends. On the outside I looked like I had it all, but inwardly I was discontent and unhappy.

Wasn't all of this success supposed to make me feel good? Wasn't it meant to give me some kind of worth and validate me as a person? Why did I still feel dissatisfied? I had a man, children, money, a career, yet none of it brought me the happiness and fulfillment I craved. I was at a complete loss. All of the things I put my hope in left me with disappointment.

Part of the problem was I had planned for a level of expectancy that never happened. Even though I had everything I longed for and set out to achieve from the time I was 18 years old, once I received it, it didn't measure up— it couldn't. I thought I had everything figured out. I tried to lay hold of every hope, dream and expectation this world offered only to come up empty.

For a long time, I allowed a world that didn't have the faintest idea how to live, tell me how to live. I bought into

> For a long time, I allowed a world that didn't have the faintest idea how to live, tell me how to live. I bought into the commercial. I believed the lie.

the commercial. I believed the lie. I was sold on the concept that this is what a perfect life is supposed to look like. So, when nothing measured up, feelings of discouragement flooded my soul. When I reached what should have been a high point in life, when everything should have been perfect, instead of celebrating, I fell apart.

When I assumed the world's way of doing things would define me as a person, and who I was meant to be, I set the stage for the ultimate sense of unhappiness. It felt awful to have put all of my hopes and dreams into something I thought would deliver great reward, only to find out that the rug had been pulled out from under me.

What should have been my greatest journey toward satisfaction, turned out to be my worst nightmare. Nothing made me happy; nothing made me whole; nothing gave me the sense of life, love and purpose I was frantically searching for. From the time I was 18, I searched for life, love and happiness in all the wrong places. In an attempt to find myself—

I lost myself. I didn't have a clue where to turn. I didn't know where to look anymore.

Believing the Lies

Even though I was falling apart emotionally and spiritually, I didn't want to admit it. Admitting my inner (wo)man was a mess meant failure. Outwardly I had it all, so how could I tell others I was miserable? I believed the lie that I had to be great, self-reliant, and perfect, or at least look like I was perfect. It wasn't okay for me to look like I had a great life and then say, "I'm not okay;" at least, not out loud. So, I lied. Every day I put on the mask that told everyone around me everything was fine, even though deep down I was anything but okay.

I kept everything locked inside and pretended; when, in reality, I was nothing more than an archetype of the walking wounded. I willingly carried heavy burdens—reluctant to unload what I diligently held in my heart every day. I worked hard at wearing the mask of confidence, outwardly convincing those around me that nothing was wrong, when inwardly I was dying. I was nothing more than a living heart donor who was secretly screaming, "Help!" while wearing a smile. I was the true actor; a true veteran of the stage. Hollywood had nothing on me. I had my act down perfectly, so perfectly that no one could tell what was really going on in my life—not even me.

There came a day, however, when I could no longer contain the by-product of my hurt and disappointment and pretend everything was good. There came a day when I could no longer put on the mask and play the role I thought I was assigned. Without warning, there came a day when a foreigner took my place on stage, someone I didn't know— someone I had never met before—and she acted nothing like me.

As a result of my outward success and my attempts at hiding the inner chaos, the people around me thought I was a class act. My friends were frequently commenting on how well I held everything together and seemed at ease while doing it. The truth of the matter was, I was a ticking time bomb, ready to explode any minute.

Sometimes, when we look at a person, we come away with an image that he/she has it all together. We can be fooled by the way she carries herself in public, by the way she speaks, dresses, or acts, coming to the conclusion that she has no problems. This is a lie. All people have problems, and no one has it all together; some are just better at wearing the mask. It's a scary thought to me now, to believe that anyone has it all together. In fact, I have learned that those, the ones who look like they have it all together, may be the very ones who are the most vulnerable. Millions of people are living with depression, yet you wouldn't know it, because they are doing their best to hide the pain. They don't want anyone to know the truth about what they are struggling with. Depression comes with a stigma, a label that no one wants to convey. Unfortunately, for some, the truth is revealed after it is too late.

A friend of mine worked with a middle-aged man, who, on the surface, looked like he had it all. He was wealthy, well-educated and well dressed. He had a lovely wife, and two grown children. He lived in an up-scale neighbor and was the CEO of the company. Yet, no one he worked with knew he battled with depression. Until one day, a perfectly normal day, filled with meetings, phone calls and a solid return on the company's investments, this man went home and shot himself. Everyone at work was stunned, completely unable to comprehend the idea that this man was anything but happy.

Another man I know just recently shared his story with me. "It was the worst year of my life," he began. In 2008, when the economy came crashing down, many people lost everything. Some lost their jobs, their homes, their financial security, and their hopes for the future. This man was no different. In order to survive he sold everything he could. His business was in trouble, but he refused to give up and desperately tried to hold onto the few employees he had. "I pretended everything was okay," he continued, "I had everyone fooled. No one knew the financial problems the company was having. I lost almost everything, but I did everything I could to hold onto my business." Before the year was out, he hit rock bottom. He was flat broke, in deep financial debt, and the company didn't earn a penny that year. Surrounded by defeat, he became so depressed he also lost the will to live. Thankfully, he survived, but not one person in his life knew the heavy burden he was carrying.

> All people have problems, and no one has it all together; some are just better at wearing the mask.

Odds are, each of us knows someone who is suffering with depression; we just aren't aware of it. We work with them, maybe even live with them, yet we miss it, completely unable to recognize the signs. Depression does give off many clues, but unless we are familiar with depression, it can go completely undetected until something drastic happens.

Just because I looked like I had it all together didn't mean I did. The people around me bought into the lie that communicated *Patty was above reproach, heartache, and the basic troubles of life,* when in reality, I wasn't ready to reveal my true self. I was afraid that if people really knew me and saw who I was underneath, they wouldn't like me anymore. So, for a long time, I, too, suffered in silence.

Truthfully, I think one of the biggest reasons I didn't open up about the depression at first was because I didn't trust anyone. I wasn't ready to become vulnerable. Vulnerability made me feel weak and frightened. I wasn't ready to allow myself to be exposed that way, to lay my soul bare before others. Deep inside, though, there was a part of me that longed for someone to listen carefully, to understand, and to willingly offer help and encouragement, to tell me everything was going to be okay. But, for a long time, I was unwilling to remove the mask, to take the risk and allow someone into my private world of pain. So, day-after-day, I continued to hide, communicating to those around me that I had a successful life and was doing just fine.

> Odds are, each of us knows someone who is suffering with depression, we just aren't aware of it.

4

The Well Was Deep

Struggling to Find a Way Out

I remember the day I began to fall into the well of depression. I was standing on stage in Dallas, Texas, before an audience of thousands, being recognized for one of the highest levels of achievement in the company. My husband was in the audience, proud of the accomplishments I had attained. Yet, as I stood on that stage, surrounded by joyful celebration and shouts of praise, I found myself thinking: *Is this all there is?* Abruptly, everything I had poured myself into that year didn't make any sense.

As I stood on that stage, listening to the loud music and thunderous applause, I began to think to myself: *Is this what I shipped my children off to a babysitter for? Is this what I did the changing of the guard with my husband for?* (When he came home from work, I went off to work. I hardly saw him that year.) In the middle of what should have been a magnificent moment, my soul began to plummet from that momentary high, to a miserable point of confusion.

On the flight home from the awards celebration, hot tears of frustration and anger welled up in my eyes. I was at the peak of success, at the height of what should have been my finest hour when I hit a wall and experienced a sense of loss that left me spiraling helplessly down a deep, dark tunnel.

In the days that followed the conference, I began to turn my back on everything and everyone I initially thought would bring me happiness. I found fault and became critical of everything my husband and children did, or didn't do. Nothing was good enough; and, no matter how hard my family tried to please me they couldn't gain my approval. And the career I once loved became pointless and felt like a huge waste of time.

> At the height of what should have been my finest hour, I hit a wall and experienced a sense of loss that left me spiraling helplessly down a deep, dark tunnel.

I wandered through each day like a blind beggar, not knowing what I was begging for. Nothing helped—no matter what I did in an attempt to feel better, it didn't work. I couldn't get over the overwhelming feelings of sadness and worthlessness. Each day became increasingly harder—every minute increasingly darker. I felt helplessly out of control, like a prisoner in my own body.

As the emotional turmoil of the depression grew, patterns of rage reemerged. In my teens years, bits and pieces of my repressed emotions surfaced, but they were nothing compared to what came out during my depression. My suppressed feelings escalated to their full potential, and it was frightening—even to me. I had never felt anything like this before. The outbursts of anger made me feel ugly, like something very dark and evil had overtaken by body. I was so enraged, at times, I felt like I could put my fist through a wall. Fortunately I didn't, but that was the level of wrath my heart and mind operated under during that time. Looking back, I justified the bouts of fury, convinced they gave me some kind of control over a situation that was completely out of control. The reality was, I was frightened and had no idea how to control anything or reverse what was ruining my life. I was confused by the emotional pain, and didn't understand where all of the negative feelings were coming from.

The one who was hit the hardest by my repressed anger was my oldest daughter. As the depression intensified, so did my bouts with rage. Often without warning, I unleashed those repressed feelings on her, often attacking her physically and verbally. The brunt of it happened while she was very young. Although, today, she claims not to remember much of the harm I inflicted on her, I believe it left a mark on her soul.

I really don't know why she was the focus of my fury and abusive nature. I didn't lash out at my other two children. For some reason, my oldest received the full frontal attack. Maybe because, like me, she was the oldest. Possibly, I saw a reflection of myself in her, a defenseless child I could take my hurt and anger out on. Perhaps I was lashing out because I saw her as the problem. Maybe I was acting out in revenge, doing to her what I wanted to do to those who had hurt me.

I never sought therapy for what I went through as a child. I never asked for professional advice about any of the repressed feelings I held on to. I was oblivious to the problem. I thought I had dealt with my past hurts and had moved on in search of a better life. But when the life I dreamed of let me down, somehow, all of the old feelings and hurts came back, flooding my soul with pain. I felt terrified, even frightened of myself. I didn't know who to turn to or what to do.

> For what seemed like an eternity, I spent my days sleeping, screaming and crying.

So when I became abusive to my daughter, I was too afraid to tell anyone. I needed help, but any time I thought about getting help, my first thought was: *They'll take her away.*

As the days dragged into months, I helplessly sank deeper and deeper into the well of depression. I spent my days sleeping, screaming and crying as a growing sense of defeat and frustration grew within my soul.

In the midst of all this anguish, alcohol became my solitary source of comfort. It wasn't much at first, just a drink or two at night after I put the children to bed. I remember sitting beside my husband watching TV, sipping a small glass of wine. Somehow, the numbing effect made me feel calmer. The effects of the alcohol were a lie. Yet, I convinced myself the alcohol had temporarily relieved the darkness.

As the rage increased and the pain of the depression became more unbearable, I had to find a way to stop it. Once I realized the alcohol made a difference in the way I felt and coped, I started to drink earlier and more often. I reached a point where I didn't want to feel anything anymore—not angry or depressed. I quickly learned alcohol was a substance I could use to help me deal with both. So, by mid-afternoon, I began to pour that first glass of numbing therapy, and continued to use it throughout the day to divert any emotional turmoil. Another advantage of the alcohol was it also made me sleepy; so, this too, became another form of escape.

A Portrait of Depression

In this section, I'm going to sidestep a little, because I would like to give you another image of depression. If you are familiar with the Bible, you may know the story found in Jeremiah, Chapter 38, when several men threw Jeremiah into a well or cistern, and left him there to starve to death. He was alone; no one was there to pull him out. The well was deep; mud filled the bottom which made it impossible for Jeremiah to free himself. With every attempt to climb out, he only sank deeper into the mud.

I know what it's like to be thrown into that deep, dark well. Into a pit where there is nothing except darkness, dirt walls and mud. I can see myself struggling to get out; fighting hard to climb the dirt walls. I can see myself clawing and digging into the sides of the clay formation, only to have pieces of dirt come lose and fall into my eyes and mouth. I'd lift one leg to try and find a foothold, only to the have the other leg plunge even deeper into the muddy floor.

I can hear myself calling out, even screaming for help. In the gloom, I hear nothing except the sound of my own voice as it echoes in the murky tunnel. Again and again I call out, but no one hears, no one comes. Soon I come to the conclusion that it is all a futile effort. There is no answer and no hope of getting out, so I sit down in the mud, surrounded by the gloomy shadows of my hollow tomb, and wait to die.

Jeremiah, trapped in the well is a perfect portrait of depression. And I could relate to him all too well. I knew how I felt when I was in that well, and I wondered if he had felt the same things I did? He must have. When he was thrown into the well, he must have been confused as to why the men put him there. He surely reasoned with them in an attempt to stop their foolishness. He must have called out, hoping someone might be passing by and would hear him. I'll bet he called out several times, day-after-day, night-after-night, with an unceasing cry for deliverance. He must have held onto the hope that one of his friends or family members would realize he was missing and search for him, and then later felt betrayed when the people in his life didn't come to his aid. Jeremiah undoubtedly tried to find a way out. I imagine he struggled to free himself. But when his efforts failed, did he, too, come to the conclusion it was a hopeless situation?

When I was in the well, I made every effort I could think of to find answers, to get better, to stop feeling the way

I did; but nothing helped. With each attempt, failure was the only outcome. It was difficult for me to come to the conclusion I couldn't help myself, or free myself from the emotional turmoil. I had to look beyond myself in order to find relief. I had to open my heart and begin to tell people something was wrong, and I needed help. This was not an easy decision. I was a private person and rarely spoke of personal matters with others; but, with the depression deepening and the rage escalating, I couldn't wait any longer. I had to take the risk. I had to ask for help.

> I made every effort I could think of to find answers, to get better, to stop feeling the way I did; but nothing helped.

No One Understood

I was afraid of what others would think. I wasn't sure how they would react when I told them about my extreme feelings of sadness and bouts of rage. Would they judge me, criticize my actions and condemn my feelings? Would they stop loving me, or stop being my friend?

Up until this point, no one, not even my husband, knew about the pain, the abuse toward our oldest daughter, or the excessive drinking—I had hidden it all too well. So, when I finally found the courage to start talking about what I was going through, to my surprise, no one judged, criticized or condemned. Instead, they simply didn't believe me. I was confused why no one took me seriously. I couldn't figure out why no one seemed to understand, or even listen.

I felt betrayed by the people I loved. Ironically, those whom I helped and supported didn't seem concerned about my problems. The pain in my heart increased every time I thought about how I had been there for them when life knocked them down. I was the bailout queen, the one everyone turned to for help in picking up the pieces of their scattered lives; yet, when I needed help, it felt like no one was there.

I recalled the countless times when I had listened, gave money, lent a hand, or offered assistance when I knew someone was in need. I wanted to help—it was the true nature of my heart. I never expected anything in return. I never gave out of duty or obligation. Yet, I cannot begin to tell you how much it hurt when I was in trouble and needed help, and no one seemed to come to my aid. In those days I felt alone, and the love in my heart grew cold. I felt cheated, and told myself that people only wanted to be around me if I had something to give. I began to push people away. I didn't want to be around people who told me they loved me one minute, and then turned their backs on me the next.

During the depression, I never felt lonelier. Even my sweet husband didn't get it. Almost every night I tried to tell him that something was wrong. And every time he would respond by saying, "Oh, you'll get over it." My husband loved me, I knew that, but he didn't understand what I was going through. He couldn't because he hadn't gone through depression himself, so he couldn't identify with the illness. Unfortunately, about seven years later, he got a crash course in understanding the full effects of depression.

My husband telling me to "get over it," never helped me "get over it." I don't know why he made that assumption, other than the fact he simply didn't understand. My husband is usually the type of guy who wants to fix everything, and his way of fixing my problem was to tell me to "get over it." But, no matter how hard I tried, I couldn't. Believe me, if I could have controlled those overwhelming feelings of anger, sadness and despair, I would have. What I needed from my husband was compassion. I needed an active listener who would give me an opportunity to be open and transparent, to really hear what I was experiencing and try to comfort me. His lack of understanding made me feel even worse, and brought on feelings of hopelessness.

Nowhere to Turn

Hopelessness—is there any word in the English language more dreadful? After I exhausted all efforts to find help through family and friends, I turned to the medical profession for relief. Although, when I first brought up the idea, my husband was totally against it. He was convinced I was fine and didn't want me to seek professional help for the simple reason it might disparage his career, or put him in a position to be discovered as having a "crazy wife." Money was tight then, because of the restorations that needed to be done on our old Victorian home, so that was another reason for him to prohibit my actions. But the lack of money, or my husband's lack of understanding, was not going to stop me. Over the next several weeks, I took every opportunity to set a little money aside. *When I have enough*, I thought, *I'll make an appointment under an assumed name and pay cash. No one would ever know.*

I remember the day I picked up the phone in order to follow through with my well-laid plan. With phonebook in hand, I began to call one doctor's office after another; bent on the mission that if I could get some pills, I'd be fine. I had a get-fixed-quick mentality. I knew I needed help, and I figured a simple prescription would do the trick. So, that day, I went down the list, calling doctor after doctor, only to hear responses like: "I'm sorry, we don't take your insurance," or, "I'm sorry, we don't handle that kind of depression."

In less than an hour, I had made my way through the entire list of professional doctors I thought could help me. Finally, when I dialed the last number on the list, a kind woman answered the phone and listened patiently to my heartfelt plea, only to tell me, at the end of our conversation, "I'm sorry, but we can't help you." As I hung up the phone a thought swiftly dawned on me: *No one can help me—I'm utterly alone. This is never going to end.* It was at that moment the darkness went deeper, and thoughts of suicide entered my mind.

The mind, when it is in a state of hopelessness, can come up with a lot of scenarios that are neither right nor healthy. When I realized there was no one who could help me, when I came to the conclusion I was totally alone and the madness wasn't going to end, I gave up. I lost hope. I sat down in the darkened gloom of my personal prison and quit trying. I told myself the only out was to die.

5

God Had Other Plans

Turning Something Bad into Something Good

Hopelessness turned into utter desperation when I realized I was completely alone in my struggle. I felt I had no friends, family, or medical support to turn to, so thoughts of suicide filled my mind. I had to do something, anything, to end the suffering. At that moment, death appeared to be the only option.

Ironically, in the days that followed, I found myself doing something I very rarely did—I prayed. I did not pray for God's help, mercy, or healing. Nor did I call on him to find answers. Rather, I asked him to take my life. He had the power to make me live or die—and I wanted to die. Every morning I prayed for the insanity to end, and every night I prayed to never wake up. I would even lie down in the afternoons with that same prayer on my mind, *Please, God, just let me die.*

I recall one day in particular. It was a sunny day in November, and I had just picked up the kids from the babysitter. As soon as I got them home I turned on a video for the girls, who were six and four years old at the time; then I took my toddler son and laid him in his crib. As soon as the kids were set, I went straight to my bedroom. I lay down on the bed, fully dressed, more than ready to die. I couldn't take it anymore, it was hell on earth, and my life was an endless misery of obscurity that I couldn't escape. As I closed my eyes, my heart again prayed for God to take my life. Instead, within seconds, I fell asleep.

> I had to do something, anything, to end the suffering. At that moment, death appeared to be the only option.

An hour later, I woke up to face the disappointment that God had not answered my prayer. Frustrated and angry that he was not filling my request, I got up grumbling at him. *Why?* I thought. *Why are you not letting me die? Surely this is not an impossible task. Can't you see how useless my life has become?*

After I had expressed my fury toward God, I looked in on my son. He was sound asleep in his crib. Downstairs, the girls were exactly where I left them, sitting quietly in front of the TV. At that moment I didn't think about the consequences of leaving three young children unattended. Now, I realize the grace and mercy that must have been at work while I was sleeping off the effects of another emotional breakdown. I believe God sent angels to watch over my children. But, in the middle of my ranting due to unanswered prayer, I couldn't recognize or appreciate the gift he had given me.

During the depression, I didn't have the capability to recognize anything good in my life. I had many wonderful things happening all around me, but I couldn't see any of it, probably because I didn't want to see it. Nor could I see the dangers of the lifestyle I had chosen in order to cope with the pain. Depression is blinding, like standing in the middle of a dark room late at night. With no light, I never saw what was right in front of me.

It was like the time I was six years old. I remember playing blind-man's-bluff on the back porch of my uncle's home. My uncle had seven children, and we were all engaged in the activity. It was nighttime, and since we didn't turn a light on, it was very dark—and of course—I was the one wearing the blindfold. And since none of us checked for hazards prior to playing the game, we didn't realize the cellar door had been left open. Cellar doors, unlike basement doors, are in the floor, not the wall. As the game progressed, I called out as my cousins taunted me toward their direction. I moved cautiously around the room; unfortunately, I wasn't cautious enough. Without warning, I stepped into the opening of the cellar and plummeted to the concrete floor below, which caused me to black out. When I woke up, Dad was carrying me up the cellar stairs.

Thankfully, I didn't suffer any permanent damage as a result of that fall, but I could have died. This incident is another portrait of depression. In the blinding darkness, you can't see anything, so you step into the well and fall helplessly to the bottom. The fall doesn't kill you, but you feel like it could, or even should, annihilate you.

During the depression, I lost a great deal. One of my biggest regrets was the time I lost with my children. I cared for my children, but I only did what was needed. My children became hostages in their own home. Other than school, I don't remember taking them anywhere or doing anything with them. I didn't play with them. I just remember popping in one video after another to keep the girls occupied, and I kept my son in his crib. I have very little record of their childhood during that time. I took all kinds of pictures of the girls when they were babies. I remember getting out the video camera and taking endless video footage; capturing lots of silly moments full of laughter and play on film—but there was nothing of my son. I was too emotionally ill to pick up a camera. I regret it now, the time and memories that we lost; but, at the time, it didn't matter—nothing mattered.

Nothing Left to Give

In the midst of my confusion, I convinced myself that everyone would be better off without me. Even though my children were very young, I believed I was doing them a favor. After all, I was making their lives a living hell. I was screaming and crying—carrying on with such fits of rage that life for them was a nightmare. Deep inside I was conflicted. I knew committing suicide was wrong and my actions would hurt my family tremendously and leave a huge void in their lives; but, the darkness was so thick and heavy, I didn't see another answer. Death seemed to be the only way any of us would find peace.

I rehearsed several different scenarios, trying to think of the best way to accomplish the goal. I have always been a strategic, well-organized woman, so this situation was no different. I needed a plan. There was a lot to consider, and I wanted to make this as easy on my family as possible.

I never actually attempted any of the scenarios I planned. I'm not sure why. Maybe deep down, I was too afraid. Plus, I really didn't *want* to hurt my family. I just wanted the madness to end—for all of us.

The most crucial point came on December 12, 1996. On this day I knew I couldn't go on one more day. When I awoke that morning, I felt my heart harden even more toward God for forcing me to face another day. I lay in bed, staring at the ceiling as if I were looking toward heaven and thought, *Why won't you let me die?*

> There was nothing left. I had reached the end of myself. And through the sobs, I began to talk to God.

Reluctantly, I got up and stepped into the shower. Hot tears poured from my eyes, mixing with the water pouring from the showerhead. Naked, drenched, and ashamed, I felt like I had been ground into the ashes from which I came. There was nothing left. I had reached the end of myself. And through the sobs, I began to talk to God. "I have nowhere else to go but you. You have to do something. No one can help me; only you can help me! Please, help me."

This was a completely different cry for relief and freedom. This time, I didn't ask him to end my life, I asked him for much more. I asked for a miracle. I knew, as I cried out, this was a desperate make-it-or-break-it moment. If God didn't do something that day, I feared I would. My plea was not an ultimatum. I wasn't bargaining with God. I had hit rock bottom. I had nowhere else to go.

> This was a completely different cry for relief and freedom. This time, I didn't ask him to end my life, I asked him for much more.

Suddenly, through the sobs, I heard what sounded like a faint voice, "Go to MOPS." (MOPS stands for Mothers of Preschoolers, a Christian women's organization that ministers to women who have children ages five and under.) At first, I moaned. I didn't want to be around people. I certainly wasn't in any mood to again put on the mask. I already belonged to the organization, so I was previously assigned to sit with a group of women. But because of the depression, I had been avoiding the meetings. As my emotions tried to persuade me to stay home, I heard it again, "Go to MOPS."

I got out of the shower, got dressed, dropped the girls off at school, and went to MOPS with my son in tow. Once there, I put on the mask that communicated to the world that I was doing fine. I was really struggling, but the last thing I wanted to do was let the ladies at the church think I wasn't doing well. I didn't want them to know about the rage and emotional turmoil, and I certainly didn't want them to know about the depression or my suicidal tendencies. Mainly, I didn't want to answer any questions. It was just easier to pretend everything was okay.

As the meeting began, I went through the motions of someone at ease. I was like an elegant dancer who had practiced her part so well, that she performed it with perfect execution. I smiled, even laughed a few times. I ate well, conversed pleasantly with the other moms, and even put together a craft. Which, by the way, I hate to do.

Toward the latter part of our MOPS gathering, the speaker came forward and stood behind the podium. She was an older woman, maybe in her mid-sixties. She was plain, with an air about her I couldn't quite put my finger on. When she began to speak, her demeanor was light and entertaining. Her mix of humor and grace caught my attention, and I found myself enjoying her tremendously. She shared some things about her life, and even talked about her husband who had Parkinson's disease. But she really gained my full attention when she shared about what it's like having a lack of joy and no real purpose in life. She didn't specifically talk about depression, but what she was saying fell right in line with what I was feeling. The real crux of her message was about finding joy and purpose in life, and that the only way to find pure joy was through Jesus. I was intrigued, and found myself hanging on her every word. As she closed, I remember her telling the group about a brochure she had, and if anyone wanted to have one to meet with her in the back of the room.

As she stepped down from the platform, I watched her make her way to the back of the room. I didn't take my eyes off her for a minute. I was utterly persuaded that I needed one of those brochures—I needed what she had offered.

Without thinking, I got up and quickly made my way to the back. She looked at me and smiled warmly. Honestly, I don't remember how the conversation started, or how I got to the point of hysterics that I did, but before I knew it, I was dumping my life at her feet. Without warning, an emotional dam broke, and I found myself rambling and sobbing uncontrollably in front of her, trying desperately to form coherent sentences.

She didn't say a word as I continued to ramble through my frantic outburst. I couldn't control what was happening. I couldn't stop crying—and I couldn't stop talking—not even when I realized that every woman in the room had turned around to stare at us. Suddenly, I didn't care. At that moment, I didn't care who knew, or what anyone thought. It didn't matter anymore. I needed help, and this woman had the answer. I was tired of holding this pain inside. I wanted out. I didn't care how—I just wanted the turmoil of this disease to end.

In the middle of all my ranting, she seemed to understand. Even though she had never met me before, I sensed she knew my pain. Somehow she knew what I was dealing with and truly wanted to help.

Quietly she listened for several minutes. Then, without saying a word, she reached out and touched me on my left arm; and when she did, the hysterics stopped. The crying and run-on sentences instantly stopped; like someone had shut off a running faucet. There was no more nausea in the pit of my stomach. The dark cloud that had been my constant companion was gone. The heaviness lifted—

everything—all of the darkness that had consumed my life was completely gone. My spirit and soul felt light, like they had taken on wings and could fly around the room. For the first time in my life, I felt free. I didn't fully understand what had happened. I was stunned and completely amazed. I stood there and stared at her, frozen by the event that had just taken place. At that moment, I had no idea if she knew or understood what had happened, because she still hadn't said a word. Yet, there was something about her I had never known before,

> I was tired of holding this pain inside. I wanted out. I didn't care how— I just wanted the turmoil of this disease to end.

and as I looked into her eyes, I could see great love and tender compassion. As I turned and walked away silently, my mind filled with thoughts as I struggled to comprehend the experience. I knew this woman did not possess the power to heal me, but I believed God did. Even though I didn't fully understand what had happened, I was convinced the power I felt rush through me that day had to be God.

Finding Freedom

When Jesus walked this earth, he brought hope wherever he went. When I asked him to help me that day in the shower, I believe he answered me by delivering me from depression. He healed me, just as he had healed so many others, and still does today. I was living in pain, darkness and despair, but when Jesus touched me everything changed. My brokenness invited him, and by acknowledging my need for him, it qualified me for his touch. I had nothing left to give but brokenness, but it was what he had been waiting for. When I removed the mask and became real with God, he heard my cry.

God wanted me to be set free from the suffering; he just had another way of ending it. I thought the only way out was death, but God had other plans. When I saw only devastation in my life—God saw promise. When I saw only hopelessness—God saw a way to bring me near. To me the depression felt like the end—to God the depression was just the beginning of a whole new life with him.

6

Coming Up from the Darkness
Release from the Pain

The week that followed, I was filled with nothing but joy. My world went from total emptiness and devastation to utter exuberance. Instantly, my life rose from the darkness and burst with delight. I had found hope. Laughter and joy returned to my heart, and a sense of pleasure overtook my soul.

A huge weight came off me the day I was delivered from depression. Jesus reached into my depraved world and turned everything right side up. My transformation was undeniable. Everyone close to me noticed. I remember one night in particular, I was standing at the stove cooking dinner when my husband called from the other room, "What's that sound?" That sound was me. I was singing! It wasn't that I was a bad singer, and he was trying to stop the awful noise coming from the kitchen. Rather, he was expressing wonder and curiosity. The joy in my voice was something he hadn't heard for a long time.

At last, things were changing in the Mason home. The atmosphere became lighter as laughter found its way in. What had once been a house full of fear, misery, anger and sadness, became a home filled with a fresh awareness of love. And those living within its walls finally felt they could begin to relax.

Another new thing that happened was I couldn't stop thinking about Jesus. This was very odd, because up until the depression, until the time I cried out to God to let me die, I didn't give him much thought. I believed in Jesus, and believed he died on the cross, but I didn't have a personal relationship with him. I rarely prayed. I never read the Bible. I only went to church when I felt like it, which was seldom. I called my friend who put Jesus at the center of her life "a fanatic." She had pictures of Jesus on her walls. His name was positioned proudly across her fireplace mantel. Christian books, along with a copy of the Bible, sat open on many tables in her home.

> A huge weight came off me the day I was delivered from depression. Jesus reached into my depraved world and turned everything right side up.

All of this made me feel uncomfortable. But after the healing, my attitude changed. I was different. In place of apathy, I became so grateful for what Jesus had done that I couldn't let go of him or the love he showed me.

The Healing Kept Coming

The growth and transformation didn't stop there. Although I was now beginning to live the life I had once dreamed about, God had more in mind. It wasn't enough for me to find his joy and peace—He wanted me to find him. He wanted me to know more than the goodness of his grace and compassion through the healing, he wanted me to know his intimate love through a personal relationship.

One week later, on December 18, 1996, Jesus brought more into my life than I would have ever thought possible. That day, I woke up with joy and a song in my heart. But that day held more—a special turning point that would leave its mark on my life forever.

At four o'clock that afternoon, my children had hair appointments at a local salon. As I waited for them, I noticed a poster on the wall advertising a Christmas play at a local church. I knew I had to go. The program was at 7 o'clock. By the time my children's haircuts were finished, it was almost 5 o'clock. Quickly, I put them in the car and drove to the church to see if tickets were still available. Since it was late in the afternoon, only the church secretary was in the office. She was a friendly woman who smiled warmly when I walked into the room.

"Do you have any tickets left for tonight's performance?" I asked.

"No, I'm sorry," she replied, "we're all sold out."

Heartbroken, I thanked her and turned to leave. But, before I crossed the threshold, the woman called out, "But come anyway; come early and we'll find you a seat."

Overjoyed, I thanked her again and told her I would do that. I hurried home and quickly made dinner for my family, got ready, and headed back to the church with my two young daughters in tow.

The church was packed. Yet, even with no tickets, the usher politely helped us find seats. The church was laid out in two main sections: a main floor and a walk-up balcony with movie theater style seating. The usher guided us to three available seats in the balcony. We sat high above the main floor and could easily see everything.

The program was broken into four unique performances. The first was a singing Christmas tree. About thirty members of the choir, all dressed in green, stood in such a way that they formed a giant Christmas tree. This group sang the newer contemporary Christmas songs. In the second portion, the singers looked like characters who had strolled off the set of a Charles Dickens adaptation of *A Christmas Carole*. The songs they sang were more traditional and time-honored. The third segment was full of childhood wonders, reminiscent of *Babes in Toyland*.

For the final act, the church reenacted the birth of Jesus. As a child growing up, I had seen the reenactment several times on television. Back then, it was acceptable to show traditional Christmas programming on the regular network stations. So, I had watched Christmas programs like *Nester the Long-Eared Christmas Donkey*, and *The Little Drummer Boy*. Yet, none of what I'd seen before touched me the way this one did. It was like I was seeing the birth of Jesus for the first time. I wept as I watched the sights and sounds. It all made me feel like I was a part of what was happening. It literally moved my soul.

When the program was over, the senior pastor took the stage and began to talk about God's grace, Jesus' redemptive love and how the only way to find salvation was through him. At the time, I had no idea what he was talking about. Although I had grown up attending a traditional church, I don't remember anyone talking about salvation in this way. I remember being called a sinner many times, but didn't realize I was separated from God due to sin. I believed Jesus died on the cross. Yet, I was unaware of the extent of the love God showed by sending his only Son to die for *me*, so I could come into an intimate relationship with him.

> I was unaware of the extent of the love God showed by sending his only Son to die for me, so I could come into an intimate relationship with him.

Until that day, my exposure to church was punitive. When my parents took me to church as a child, I remember the priest standing up front calling all of us sinners. I didn't understand the allegation, so his accusations only made me mad. Church, in my eyes, was not a place to find love and acceptance. Rather, it was a place of burdensome rules and mechanical rituals. Church intimidated me, and I often left feeling worse than when I arrived. So, when I became old enough to make my own decisions, I only went on holidays and rare occasions.

But now, I felt different. I saw God with a new perspective. So when the pastor asked if anyone wanted to receive Jesus as his/her personal Savior, I said "yes." My response was not out of duty or obligation, or even a sense of gratitude. At that very moment, I had absolutely no idea what all of this meant—all I knew, all I understood, was I needed Jesus, and that was enough.

Without hesitation, as the pastor prayed, I responded, echoing his every word. Heavy tears streaked my face as I opened my heart to receive Jesus into my life. It was a moment in time I will never forget, an enduring moment that changed me forever. Just like the healing, saying "yes" to Jesus was a new beginning, a fresh start in a life that was once drowning in darkness.

Since That Day

Since that day, Jesus changed my heart, old attitudes, and life in ways I never dreamed possible. He took all my striving, all my efforts to find happiness and self-worth, and offered me something of greater value. I went from looking for love in all the wrong places—to knowing true love (1 John 4:16). I went from wearing the mask, trying to be perfect in a flawed world—to resting in the assurance that I am fearfully and wonderfully made (Psalm 139:14). I went from having no hope—to having a hope and a future (see Jeremiah 29:11). For years I thought in order to find myself I had to find someone or something to fill me—a man, children, money, travel, a successful career. It felt like a part of me was missing, and I didn't know where or how to find it. For 17 years I went on one quest after another in an attempt to find what my soul longed for; but, each time I went out in search of what I thought I was missing, I ended up disappointed and empty. This world had nothing to offer me; and every time I allowed the world, and its views, to fill me in some way, the results were unsatisfying and only left an ache in my soul.

What I have learned is that God created us to have an intimate relationship with him. When God formed each of us, he created us with a God-sized void that only he can fill. We can search the whole world; try everything we can think of to fill that void. But, every time we do, we will come away empty and unsatisfied. Oh, we may find temporary quick fixes that give us a false sense of satisfaction, but it doesn't take long for the momentary thrill to wear off, and send us right back to feeling hungry again.

> Jesus changed my heart, old attitudes, and life in ways I never dreamed possible.

From the day Jesus came into my life, the relationship we share has continued to grow closer and deeper. As a result, I have found meaning in life and a reason to live. I found purpose. My life has direction; a true sense of determination that is leading me down paths I never dreamed I would take. For example, if you told me, prior to the depression, I would one day be an author and speaker, and be involved in women's ministry, I probably would have laughed. Even though I didn't see myself this way, God did. He knew the plans he had for me long before I was born. He knew what he desired to accomplish in my life, and he knew the path I would have to take to find my way to those purposes. God knew, from the beginning, how to win my heart, draw me close to him, and bring me into the plans he had for me.

Once upon a time I was Jeremiah, unwillingly thrown into a deep, dark well with no way out. But, like Jeremiah, I didn't die in that well, although I thought I would. The Bible doesn't tell us how long Jeremiah was trapped in the well, but we do learn that at some point the king heard about Jeremiah and sent thirty men to tie rags together and pull him out (see Jeremiah 38:10-13). Just like Jeremiah, the day came when my helper tied rags together, reached into the darkness, and pulled me out. And when I came out of that well, I came out a different person. Since then, Jesus has shown me how to tie those rags together so I can bring hope to other Jeremiahs, showing them God's love and grace. The power of God's love delivers hope, healing and freedom to a weary soul. In Christ there is liberty, a freedom and sense of wholeness that only comes from him.

Does God Really Care?

Right now, you may be asking: *Does God really care about me?* Sometimes it's hard to see the truth that God really does care about you personally. Sometimes, when you have been through so much, it's hard to wrap your mind around the reality that God loves you and has a plan and purpose for your life, too.

When God originally created this world, it was perfect. There was no pain, no disease, no death, and no depression. But when man turned away from God and turned toward his own way, sin entered the perfect world God created, which, in turn, caused a ripple effect, bringing all kinds of suffering into the world. But God wants to restore what was lost, and he longs to restore the relationship he once shared with man in the Garden of Eden. That's why God sent Jesus, his one and only Son, to die for you and me, to take our sins upon himself, so we can be forgiven, find healing from our wondering, and be brought into the relationship that he longs to share with each of us (see Isaiah 53:4-5).

God loves you and cares about you. He watches over you, and longs for the moment you will give your heart to him. He sees your pain. He knows every tear you cry—and he knows the longing of your soul to find freedom.

I'm not trying to preach to you. I am a simple woman who found love, acceptance and healing through the heart of a Savior who was willing to save her. My purpose is to share the love and hope I've found. I know what happens to a heart that is locked up in emotional chains, and I know the freedom that can only come from Jesus. You are not alone, reach out to Jesus. Take off the mask. Invite him into all the areas of your brokenness by acknowledging your need for him. Open your heart and ask him to give you hope. Ask him to help you overcome depression, and to teach you how to live in him.

7

Overcoming Depression

Learning to Live Again

God wants to heal and restore you. He wants you to be free from depression; but, it is important to understand that God is sovereign. The way he chooses to deliver you from this pain, and the time frame in which he chooses to release you, is completely in his hands. God is a God of miracles. As in my case, he can reach out and heal you in an instant. However, please recognize God's primary purpose is to bring wholeness, to bring you close to him, so he may not heal you the same way he healed me. But be assured, he can do anything, if you give him the opportunity.

My first step toward finding emotional freedom was to allow myself to get real with God. Before God could deal with the depression and the emotional turmoil that was holding me captive, I had to be authentic with him. That day in the shower, I released all the pain I was feeling. I sobbed through every word, but I laid my heart bare. I allowed myself to be vulnerable. I admitted my need for God and acknowledged that only he could help me. I believe my sincere heart was the key he had been waiting for to unlock my prison door.

God invites each of us to give him our burdens. In First Peter 5:7 it says, "Cast all of our anxiety on him because he cares for us." To cast means to throw off with force, to eject; to get it far away. To cast does not mean to toss gently or lay the offense down. If we only lay it down it's far too easy to pick it back up again. We want the depression, and all of the emotional pain we carry, to be as far away from us as possible. God wants us to cast all of our burdens upon him.

God desires to not only set us free, but to get to the source of our pain, emotional turmoil and suffering. Depression is often the evidence that something else is going on, that there are underlying problems which still need to be dealt with. When God released me from depression it was only the starting point of a journey toward restoration. God knows the work and restorative healing that needs to be done in each of us. He knows how to restore us—mind, body, soul and spirit. He knows how to get to the root of the matter.

Getting to the Root of the Matter

When God touched my life, he gave me a new song, a fresh purpose and restored hope. But, that didn't mean I had nothing but good days from then on. Even though the depression itself was gone, *the wounds ran deep*. I was still carrying emotional baggage: roots of anger, fear and insecurity from childhood that were imbedded deep within my soul. And that, my friend, has been a journey toward freedom.

The crippling effects of depression had been lifted, but I still needed to get to the root of my emotional baggage and go through the process of restoration. I had to learn to trust God with the origin of not only my depression, but the origin of all the repressed anger and fear I had been harboring. I had to open my heart again and expose myself to the work that needed to be done. I needed to reach a point where I was no longer willing to cover up the problems. If I was going to be *finally free*, I had to allow God to get to the root of the matter so I could be free from not only the symptoms, but also the cause.

As I began to allow God to take me through this process toward emotional freedom, I began to recognize how my emotions affected me, whether positively or negatively, and I learned to never underestimate the events of my past, even if they seemed trivial. These events had an effect on my soul, and, over time, these hurts found a way to surface. Also, because I didn't deal with my emotions effectively, I unknowingly allowed them to fester and grow stronger. I thought I had put them behind me by either pretending they didn't exist, or by moving on convincing myself I had gotten over these feelings, when in reality I was only covering them up.

> Before God could deal with the depression and the emotional turmoil that was holding me captive, I had to be authentic with him.

Over the years, even prior to the depression, there were plenty of indicators informing me something was wrong, that

I was carrying emotional roots of anger, resentment, fear and insecurities, low self-esteem and shame. And these warning signs would surface every time something happened to trigger a suppressed memory or feeling. In an instant, that seemingly small event would throw me back into a place where old feelings of hurt, anger and resentment would resurface. When this happened, something I thought I had gotten over would wash over me, bringing with it a tidal wave of emotion.

> When God touched my life, he gave me a new song, a fresh purpose and restored hope.

I cannot tell you how many times I had emotional breakdowns or lost my temper over the simplest things, little things that left people scratching their heads. It was because the root, which had not been dealt with yet, needed to be removed. In order to let go, move forward and find freedom I had to confront my past, I had to face the fact that I was covering up the problem instead of dealing with it. I could no longer ignore the problem or pretend it didn't exist. That was like putting a Band-Aid on a broken bone.

Every negative emotion has a root, and these roots don't just go away. They have to be extracted. Since I hadn't faced my roots of emotion, I suffered greatly, and caused others to suffer. I allowed my emotions to dictate my actions, which ultimately directed my life. By not properly dealing with my emotions and getting to the root of the matter, I put myself in a state of emotional bondage.

Think of it this way, emotions are like the dandelions that grow in your yard. You can mow over them so they no longer appear in the lawn, but a couple of days later, if they haven't been removed from the root, they come back.

In order to allow the removal procedure to begin, I had to reach a point where I was no longer going to allow my past hurts to define me. I had to say, "Enough! I'm done! I don't want to feel this way anymore. I don't want to live this way anymore!"

I recall the day I made up my mind that I was no longer going to be controlled by anger. It was right after I had unexpectedly blown up at two very good friends. At the time this happened, I assumed they would understand my bout of anger and be compassionate. I thought they would lovingly put their arms around me in an effort to help me understand why I was so upset. They didn't. Instead, my outburst caught them off guard. They were so stunned by my emotional explosion, for a time, they didn't want anything to do with me.

The day after this outburst, I got on my knees and told God to get to the root of my anger. "Whatever it takes," I prayed. "Get rid of this anger!" I had reached a point where I wanted that vile root gone. I wanted to stop holding on to the harmful influences. I wanted to stop being controlled by my emotions; to give up the bad behaviors in order to receive something good. I reached a point where I was willing to face the pain of my past instead of running from it. I finally got to where I was willing to turn over every wrong and place it in the hands of love.

The Journey of Restoration

The process of getting to the root of the matter is not easy, nor is it automatic. I'm still going through the process. At first, it was agonizing as God showed me the origin of the roots I had allowed to fester throughout life. As he touched my shattered heart, it was painful because I found myself, once again, revisiting a part of my past. This process caused old feelings to resurface which triggered old emotions and revealed past scars.

I'm not going to lie, I didn't like this process; but, I wanted to be *finally free*, so I had to face some things I didn't want to face. I needed to reexamine old wounds and allow them to become visible. The difference was, unlike losing control and allowing my emotions to surface in a negative way, this process helped me to face the pain in the light of God's love, so he could take that pain and turn it into something good.

It is human nature to think this will be an easy escape. We think being set free will be pain free. We don't realize that once Jesus opens the door to our personal prison cell, we still have to walk out of that prison.

There is no easy way out of the emotional bondage. At times, I've struggled greatly, but in order to get through the struggle, I cling to God. No matter what happens or how I feel going through this process, I cling to the knowledge that he is exchanging my imbedded roots for something much sweeter. I know as he takes each piece of my shattered heart, he will give it back to me anew. He is taking what I've suffered and giving me hope. He is taking my bondage and giving me freedom. He is taking my feelings of death and giving me life.

The beauty of being instantly delivered from depression was that I found hope, and hope gave me the will to fight. After tasting the devastation, it felt incredible to be released and finally unshackled from those heavy chains. God gave me a great gift when he delivered me from the darkness and saved me, but there was still a lot of work that needed to be done in my heart, mind and soul. The battle may have been won, but the war wasn't over. And through it all, day-by-day, God wants me to continually give him everything. He wants to take my wounded past and exchange it for a brighter future. He wants to set me free from the things that hold me captive and teach me how to live.

> God gave me a great gift when he delivered me from the darkness and saved me, but there was still a lot of work that needed to be done in my heart, mind and soul.

How about you? Are you ready to get to the root of the matter? Are you are ready to turn over everything you've been trying to hide? Are you ready to bring every burden, every feeling of bitterness, resentment, and anger, whatever you are holding on to? Are you ready to bring it all to God so He can exchange it for something much sweeter? Are you ready to receive his joy, peace and love? If so, then share your heart with Jesus.

Restoration Isn't Renovation

Restoration is not renovation. When you renovate something you fix it, but when something is restored, it is put back to its original state. Believe me, you don't want to be fixed, you want to be restored. You don't want to settle for an overhaul—you want to be whole. Don't say to God, "Fix me." Say, "Restore me!" When Jesus comes back and makes all things new (see Revelation 21:5), He is going to restore what was lost—He is not going to fix it. He is going to put everything back to its original state.

Several years ago, my husband and I renovated a 100-year-old historical Victorian gem; although it didn't look like a gem at first. The house sat vacant for over a year. The prior owners of twenty years didn't take care of it at all. So, by the time we tried to obtain it, it was considered to be in condemned condition. Even though the foundation was good, the city officials wouldn't let us take occupancy. Their plan was to tear the old girl down, and build a parking lot for the growing businesses that surrounded the property. After several meetings, phone calls, and trips to city hall, the city officials finally conceded and allowed us to close on the house.

Once we moved in, we were hit with many unexpected issues and problems. We knew, up front, that the roof leaked and that the shutters were barely attached. We saw the overgrown landscaping that covered the house, and how desperately it needed a paint job. The inside of the house was worse, overrun by years of decay and neglect. Dust and cobwebs covered everything standing; and a cantankerous odor filled the rooms with the stench of death. When we bought the house, we knew about the things we could see, but there were many other hidden problems that were not obvious until we began the restoration process. The extra work this process caused was not something we foresaw or planned for, but once these buried flaws were exposed, we were able to deal with them. In the end, the house turned out better than we originally hoped.

This is what restoring a life can look like if you allow Jesus (the Master Carpenter) to purchase your condemned house with the sole purpose of restoring its beauty. If you put an end to your plans to just tear the thing down, and allow Jesus to restore you, you will be better than you ever hoped or imagined. He will deal with the years of neglect, sweep the house clean and remove the unwanted debris from your life. Jesus will uncover things you either didn't know about, or issues you've held onto for years and tried to hide. This can be a painful process and something you didn't plan on. But when it is all said and done, you will become more beautiful than you ever imagined.

While my husband and I worked on that dilapidated old house, we also caught the attention of those around us. The neighbors took note, and they too began to refurbish their homes. The local news caught wind of what we were doing and interviewed us a couple of times. Word spread that this old house was getting more than a facelift, and people came from near and far to see the results. One Christmas, we even opened the house for public tours to raise money for a community project. We were amazed at how many people came, and by the comments they made as they saw each room. Everyone who visited that old house was completely amazed at the fresh appearance of life it reflected. It was better than new—it was restored.

Each of us, in our condemned state, is like this raggedy old Victorian. But, when the Master Carpenter comes and moves in, regardless of our prior condition, he begins a process of restorative transformation. Many of us don't realize what is inside or the damage that has been done, until he begins the cleaning and rebuilding process. But, if we allow the work to be done, we can become a glorious masterpiece, a work of art that others will marvel at.

> You don't want to be fixed, you want to be restored. You don't want to settle for an overhaul—you want to be whole.

Don't be afraid. Most of us spend too much time running from everything that makes us feel uncomfortable. Restoration means new life. God wants to get out of you what he put into you. God intends to undo, overdo, and outdo any evil or wrong done to you, but you need to allow him to do the work of restoration.

Jesus is the Master Carpenter you can count on to get the job done, and to do the job right. If you let him, he will bring forth incredible beauty from the brokenness and ashes. God's greatest work comes when you come to the end of yourself, and then give him all the broken pieces. If you don't run from what he desires to do in you, he will begin the construction effort that will bring about wholeness and restoration.

72   Finally Free

Release from Darkne
and Freedom for the C?

Jesus came to bind up the broken'
prisoners free. He came to provide for thos⌣
turn the pain of their ashes into something beauɯ⌣
came to strip away the sackcloth of despair and clothe them
in royal garments of praise, to place a crown of beauty upon
their heads—to adorn them. Jesus came to reveal himself,
his favor, his grace, mercy, and personal love. He came to
bring healing and freedom to lost and hurting souls. He came
to restore the places long since devastated, and to rebuild
what was stolen and destroyed. He came to bring healing
and forgiveness, so you and I can find what our souls truly
long for and crave (see Isaiah 61:1-4).

Jesus wants to set you free, but that may mean you may
have to face some things you don't want to face. Restorative
healing is a process that will cause old wounds and feelings
to resurface, and you may not be ready to either deal with
them or let them go. I know it is challenging to let go of the
past, to stop harboring resentment and anger. Sometimes, it
seems easier to hold onto the pain than to forgive someone
who harmed you. But finding freedom means being released
from whatever is holding you captive. This may mean letting
go of a troubled past or forgiving yourself for mistakes you
have made. You may need to learn to stop worrying or playing a certain scenario over and over again as if somehow the
past could be changed. It may mean letting go of anger and
bitterness by forgiving someone—someone who may have
brought you great harm. This is the price for freedom, but

don't let the cost outweigh victory. The things that
d you captive don't have to keep you bound one more
day.

When Jesus releases us from darkness, he sets us free from the world's views, the lies of the enemy, and the violation of a painful past. He sets us free from the wrongs that have been done to us, and the afflictions that have tried to destroy us. Jesus throws open those doors of freedom, shines his light into the darkness and illuminates real truth and love. However, whether or not we remain free will depend on us.

Some people, after Jesus unlocks their prison door, choose to remain in that cell, fearful of coming out. Others momentarily taste the freedom only to put themselves right back in jail. Why? Why would anyone allow themselves to be held captive in a man-made prison?

Usually we remain a captive because we haven't allowed God to finish the work he has begun. We don't permit him to bring complete restoration. We don't give him the opportunity to rebuild the ancient ruins and restore the places that were devastated (see Isaiah 61:4). Another reason we keep ourselves imprisoned is because we refuse to forgive or let go of hurts. We continue to harbor harmful attitudes and grievances, allowing them to consume us. We carry roots of anger, resentment, bitterness, hatred, even depression, refusing to tell these roots, "Good riddance!" This is a stronghold of emotional bondage.

> Whether or not we remain free will depend on us.

A stronghold is a recurring pattern that leaves behind feelings of hopelessness and defeat. It's any lie, attitude, action, or emotion that takes control of our lives over and over again. A stronghold is a yoke, a burden or hindrance that will weigh us down, and, eventually, even destroy us if it's not dealt with.

The good news is Jesus wants to take those strongholds, our yokes of burden, and exchange them for his yoke which is easy and light (see Matthew 11:28). He wants to give us freedom for our souls. He wants to break off every yoke that is not of him and put on us his yoke of freedom. He wants to break off every lie we are buying into, every attitude that has us bound and exchange them for truth.

The Things that Hold Us Captive

One such stronghold that keeps many of us bound is unforgiveness. To some of us, forgiveness is an ugly word. In our minds, forgiving the one who has wronged us communicates that what that person did is okay. The offense he/she caused is okay. The abuse is okay. The rape is okay. The betrayal is okay—but it's not okay. No matter what he/she did, it's not okay. If someone harmed you it's not okay. Forgiving someone from your heart doesn't make what they did okay; rather, it opens a door, giving you an opportunity to be okay.

Forgiving someone who has harmed you never means what he/she did was acceptable. It doesn't right the wrong. It doesn't change the situation or erase it from your memory. Exercising forgiveness allows you to be permanently set free from the festering roots of hate, resentment, anger and fear which are the results of those hurtful actions. Forgiveness grants you a lifelong get-out-of-jail-free card. Forgiveness keeps you from being thrown back into that jail cell.

In Matthew 18:21-35 we learn that unless a person forgives from the heart he will be thrown into prison and tortured. When we do not forgive from that deep place within our hearts, the pain of resentment and anger grows and gnaws at us, continually tightening the chains that keep us in turmoil—now that's emotional torture.

Forgiving from the heart is hard. Most of us can achieve an intellectual level of forgiveness on our own, but forgiveness at the heart level is a whole different story. Many of us can say, "I forgive you," and think we mean it, but unless the issue is dealt with at the heart level by getting to the root of the matter, we'll never reach that place of forgiveness where we find healing and freedom for our souls. Only God can help us get to that place of forgiveness.

> Only God can help us get to that place of forgiveness.

Right now you may be thinking: *What a minute, I've done nothing wrong! Why should I be the one to forgive?* What happened may not have been your fault. You didn't ask for the offense, nor did you do anything to provoke it, however, the original hurt someone caused you is only half the problem.

Harboring any wrongdoing in your heart will eat away at you like a cancer. Harboring an offense, carrying it in your heart like a bitter memory, will keep you locked up in an emotional prison. So, even though none of this may be your fault, forgiveness is an important step toward finding freedom and being released from the past.

I understand that when someone has wronged us, hurt us deeply, even hurt someone we love, it is hard not to take matters into our own hands and try to bring about vindication. It is human nature to want to lash out, to be angry, resentful, and full of unforgiveness. We want the person who hurt us, or hurt our loved one, to suffer. Somehow, this course of action justifies our suffering. An eye for an eye—right? But the truth of the matter is: Being unforgiving and vengeful only increases the pain.

Remember, not taking vengeful actions, or forgiving someone for any harm he/she caused, doesn't indicate what he/she did is okay. Forgiving someone from your heart makes you okay. God knows what you've been through. He knows all the pain you've suffered, and he does want to vindicate you. However, in order to receive justification, freedom, and healing you need to release these things into his hands. Rest from your actions and attitudes to get even—rather, rest in God, give him the room to act on your behalf. Allow him to give you comfort in your mourning, joy in your grief, and hope for despair. Invite him to restore the devastated places and to rebuild what was stolen and destroyed.

For years I felt hurt and angry over the physical and emotional abuse I suffered as a child, but I never dealt with those harmful emotions. I tried to hide them, move forward and even pretend that the abuse never happen; but, holding in all of that repressed hurt and anger was like standing beneath a volcano that was about to erupt. The mountain looked pretty from the outside, but inside it was nothing but hot, molten lava that would one day explode. Repressed emotions eventually surface. When they do, it is like a tsunami hitting the shores of an Island. They often hit hard and fast. There is nowhere to run, and these emotions leave few survivors.

In order to find freedom from all of the hurt and pain from my past, I had to forgive. I had to forgive my dad, the kids at school and all the people who hurt me over the years. I recall the day I finally forgave my dad. (It was after I invited Jesus into my life.) I was at a point where I was enjoying my newfound liberty from depression, but I was only beginning to go through the restoration process. That morning, as I went about my day, a thought came to mind: *Tell him you love him*. At first, I wasn't sure who "he" was. No one in particular came to mind. Then, suddenly, as the thought, *Tell him you love him*, came to mind a second time, I thought of my dad.

Dad's reaction, the first time I told him I loved him, was not at all what I expected. He hugged me with tears in his eyes and told me he loved me, too. From that time on, he hugged me every chance he got. While growing up, I could count on one hand the number of times Dad hugged me— now he hugs me all the time. We talk, laugh, play games together, and share thoughts and conversations we never would have before.

I know what I am describing might sound far too simple, maybe even impossible that a broken relationship could be repaired so quickly, but what I didn't realize until then was my dad was hurting too. He was no different than me. He was simply another wounded soul looking for love. Before that day, I never took the time to get to know my father. I didn't realize all of what he had been through, all of what he had suffered. Dad never apologized for the abuse, I never asked him to. But after hearing his story, I understood my dad in a way I never understood him before. Plus, understanding his past gave me a great deal of insight into mine, and why he treated me and my brother the way he did.

I can't fully explain what happened the day I told dad I loved him, but suddenly I was able to forgive him. Not because he deserved my forgiveness, or because it now gave me some kind of newfound power over him. Instead, it was because it allowed me to open my heart. This type of compassion gave me a release I had never known before. Forgiveness gave me the opportunity to heal. It didn't right the wrong—I was still abused—but the abuse no longer had as much power over me. Over time, as I continued to go through the restoration process, I got stronger. Fear and insecurity didn't hold me captive as much, and the repressed anger didn't surface nearly as often. Am I perfect? No. But now I understand the source, and with God's help, we are getting to the root of the matter. Daily I am being restored. I am in the process of finding deep, emotional healing. Forgiving my dad and telling him I loved him was a huge step toward that healing.

> In order to find freedom from all of the hurt and pain from my past, I had to forgive.

If you are the one you need to forgive, allow me to encourage you to take this step. Maybe you feel responsible for the place where you now find yourself. Perhaps the things you've tried to keep quiet have haunted your soul. There are many choices we make; some may even cause us to feel shame or self-hatred. However, just as unforgiveness toward others holds us bound, so does not forgiving ourselves for the choices and mistakes we've made.

I've had many regrets in life, and perhaps the biggest one is how I saw life during the depression. I made choices, said things, did things, and acted in ways that placed a mark of shame on my soul. To embrace freedom, I had to admit my mistakes and forgive myself for all of the hurt and pain I had imposed on others.

For example, as I confronted the way I had unleashed my repressed anger upon my oldest child, it broke my heart. I lamented at how I lashed out at her. Yet, I had to come to a place where I could forgive myself and also ask for her forgiveness. She was very young, but I recall the day I shared my heartfelt remorse with her. Immediately, she began to cry as she threw her arms around my waist and said, "I didn't think you loved me."

> To embrace freedom, I had to admit my mistakes and forgive myself for all of the hurt and pain I had imposed on others.

I had to forgive myself for all the choices I made, like drinking while my children were around, or leaving them unattended while I went to sleep off another dark day of depression. I had to forgive myself for the desire to take my own life and leave my family behind to deal with the loss and aftermath. I had to forgive myself for all of the things I regretted, to let myself move forward, and to allow my family and God to forgive me.

At first, I must admit, this was hard to do, because at the time I didn't fully understand God's mercy and grace. I couldn't see how a holy and righteous God could possibly offer me anything but condemnation and judgment for the things I had done. But after Jesus came into my life, he began to show me the true heart of God and that he didn't condemn me for any of the mistakes I made. He didn't treat me as my sins deserved; instead he showed me kindness and gentleness (see Psalm 103:8-10). Once I accepted God's heart toward me, and began to understand the measure of his love, I was able to forgive myself and receive his forgiveness.

Receiving a revelation of God's love toward me was paramount—it changed everything. Realizing how much God loved me and sent his Son to die for me, to take the punishment for my poor choices (see John 3:16), awakened my soul to receive God's forgiveness. Accepting God's forgiveness somehow gave me the ability to forgive in a way I couldn't before. God's love and forgiveness is beyond my comprehension; but, the wonderful thing is, I don't have to figure it out—I only need to receive it. And when I do, God fills my heart with his love, helping me to forgive both myself and others, even when it is difficult.

If you are weary of carrying emotional strongholds and yokes of oppression, all of the burdens that have kept you suppressed and worried about life, give them to Jesus. Ask him to break off every hindrance, fear, lie, attitude and habit keeping you in emotional bondage. Ask him to dig deep, and pull out every root of emotional bondage imbedded in your soul (see Matthew 15:13). Ask Him to help you to forgive yourself and the people who hurt you. Ask him to begin the restoration process, so he can turn your life into something beautiful.

8

Hope for the Future

Discovering Fresh Purpose and Life

For what seemed like an eternity, my soul drowned in anguish. At a point when I was unable to go on, I cried out to God. I turned to the only One I believed could save me, even though I didn't know him personally. At that time, I had no idea why God would find it in his heart to save someone as messed up as me. Nonetheless, at my lowest point, he came into the turmoil of my personal madness and set me free from depression. Also, when he set me free, he gave me a miraculous and powerful testimony—a testimony of hope, of love and deliverance, of healing power and his unfathomable grace.

As God continued to work in my life, I began to realize something remarkable—God had a specific plan for my life (Jeremiah 29:11). He wanted to release me from past emotional bondage, so he could give me a purpose for the future. All the pain I had gone through had a purpose. Never, in my wildest dreams, would I have guessed God wanted to use what I had been through as a light in dark places. Yet, here I was with a song of testimony and praise. And, he has taken that testimony and used it many times over the years, giving me opportunities to share with various groups, churches, and women's organizations.

Each time I share, I watch with awe and wonder at the work God does in the hearts of those who hear my story. One time, I had an entire audience break down and weep with renewed hope when they connected with my story. Some I have seen set free on the spot, as they opened their hearts to receive God's mercy and deliverance. Others have come up to me afterward to share how God touched them and offered them a new sense of optimism and hope. Each group is different, I never know what to expect; but, whenever I am given the opportunity to share my story, I witness some form of God's incomparable mercy and grace.

> Never, in my wildest dreams, would I have guessed God wanted to use what I had been through as a light in dark places.

God wants you to know that he has a plan for your life, too. He wants to set you free and fill your heart with his love, fill all the empty places, so you have something to celebrate. He wants to redeem your past and give you a powerful testimony. His goal is to give you hope for the future. A new song waits for you; a song that will sing boldly of his love and mercy—one you can share with those he places around you.

Do not be ashamed or afraid of what others may think when they hear about your less than perfect life. Tell your story! Allow God to take that pain, turn it around, and use it. I call it: *Nightmare to Ministry*, and I often speak on the subject. *Nightmare to Ministry* happens when God uses the worst part of our lives in order to bring out the best part of us. God took me from the pit of depression, the one thing I despised more than anything in my life, and used it far beyond anything I could have imagined.

In the midst of your circumstances, at the height of your worst nightmare, God says, "I choose you." Not in spite of your past, but because of it. God wants to take your worst nightmare, redeem it, restore it, and use it—not only for His glory, but for the encouragement and support of others who are still suffering.

Everyone experiences trials and hardships. No one is exempt. God has a plan and purpose for every experience in life. Every man and woman I know, especially those who share their stories openly with others, have had something in their past that motivates their future. For example, Charlotte Hunt, wrote a book called *Damaged Goods: Learning to Dream Again*[iv]. In her book, she shares her traumatic past of physical and sexual abuse, and her struggle to find love and acceptance. Her heartwrenching trials led her to depression and seven suicide attempts until God redeemed her past in order to give her a powerful present and future. Now, through her book and speaking, she shares with audiences all over the world, helping them to let go of their painful past by teaching them to dream again.

My friend, Sheryl Griffin, wrote a book called, *A Scarlet Cord of Hope: My Journey Through Guilt, Shame, and Fear to Hope*[v]. Through her story, Sheryl shares about her painful past with alcoholic parents, an abusive first marriage, and abortion. The effects of these events, coupled with the choices she made throughout life, brought on overwhelming feelings of shame which caused her to begin having severe panic and anxiety attacks. But, in the midst of her suffering, God showed Sheryl how to put together the puzzle pieces of her life by helping her grasp his scarlet cord of hope, instead of the cords that tried to snare her. Now Sheryl shares her story openly, wanting others to know they are not alone, and that they do not have to be entangled by the emotional cords of guilt, fear, and shame.

Another precious woman I know has been battling cancer, along with her two sons, for the past 18 years. Between the three of them, they have been diagnosed many times, undergone years of chemotherapy and numerous surgeries to remove cancerous nodes, including amputation. After a long battle, her youngest son Joshua passed away at the age of 16. Her older son, Christopher, continues to fight for his life after recently undergoing surgery to replace the bones in his infected arm and leg.

Yet, throughout this journey, she remained a constant advocate for her sons, by encouraging them and lifting their spirits. "Together," she says, "we learned to face every challenge with an open heart, to live joyfully, and to laugh and smile as much as possible. We have learned that life here on earth is not the end, and each moment is a gift."

Today, Teresa Rose shares her family's story every chance she gets, letting people know how God is using her circumstances to help and encourage others. She knows and understands the power of her testimony. By sharing with others, it has given her a sense of purpose and renewed hope. She recognizes the message of inspiration God is sending through her.

A young man, during his college years, became homeless. Today he is off the streets and employed as a social worker, helping the struggling children and families of his community. "I am grateful," he says, "for the days of poverty." His experience of living in destitution has not only become a personal banner of courage and self-determination, but an incredible opportunity to understand and assist others who are hurting as he once did.

> At the height of my depression, the last thing I would have wanted to do was help someone else, especially someone with depression.

Right now you might be thinking, *I don't have it in me to be a spokesperson to bring hope and healing to anyone.* I understand. At the height of my depression, the last thing I would have wanted to do was help someone else, especially someone with depression. I was the one who needed help. In the midst of my suffering, the darkness blinded me to any sort of purpose. I couldn't see anything good coming from my present circumstances. The truth was I wanted to get as far away from the pain as possible and never look back.

When we are going through a hard situation the pain is often more than we can carry ourselves. At that point, we don't have any energy to help others because all we can think about is how badly we need help. We aren't able to see or understand that there is purpose in the madness. We can't grasp how any sort of healing can take place when we begin to help others. As a result, we start to feel we could never help anyone else, or we believe we would have to be completely whole before we can offer hope to another soul.

I am living proof God can and will redeem a harmful past in order to give a bright future. I wasn't completely whole when he began to use me. When I shared my testimony publicly for the first time, I had only begun to go through the restoration process. I didn't have all the answers. I didn't even fully understand all of what God wanted to do with my testimony, but I knew I had one. I knew I had a powerful story of deliverance through a miraculous healing, and I was invited to tell it. Each time I did, God moved in the hearts of others.

That's all you need to do is share your story—talk about what you know. If you let him, God can lift you from the pit and give you a voice and a passion to help those who are hurting. You don't have to be perfect to share your story; you just need to be willing.

One of the reasons I think it is easy for me to talk about my depression and the pain of my past is because every time I do, another piece of my heart is rebuilt. Every time I stand before an audience and share my testimony, even as I share my story with you through this book, I see God's goodness in my life, and I am renewed. With every life I see changed, I am blessed beyond words that my story has helped another person find hope for the future.

I'll never forget the first time I shared about my battle with depression and God's miraculous grace. It was about 6 months after he touched my life, and about two months after I had prayed a prayer asking God for two things. First, I asked him to never let me forget where I came from. Secondly, I asked him to let me be a vessel he could use. I wanted to give back, to be a vehicle through which he could bring hope to others like he did for me, even if it was for

> God can lift you from the pit and give you a voice and a passion to help those who are hurting.

only one woman. So, in answer to my prayer, that night, after the event, a woman came up to me and told me I must be an angel of God. Of course I'm not, but in her eyes, God had answered her prayer. He heard her cry for help, and through me he had answered her.

In that moment, this dear sweet woman opened her heart and shared about the devastating year she had gone through. She had lost her husband, her only son, her mother and her dog all in one year. But when she heard my testimony and the power of God's instant healing upon my life, it gave her new hope. She no longer felt helpless or hopeless —she felt the love of a God she thought had forsaken her.

The ironic thing was she didn't even know the church where I was speaking existed. It wasn't a small church, but it was out on a country road, away from the city. She told me she was so depressed and lonely that she was on her way to commit suicide by driving her car off a bridge. Instead, she found herself at the church. She said when she saw all the cars in the parking lot, curiosity got the better of her, and she decided to come in. She had no idea what the event was, or what she was about to hear, but God directed her path. Once inside, she heard me talking up front, and was drawn in by my story.

Angie didn't commit suicide that night. In fact, I wrote to her for a long time afterward, sharing letters about God's grace and healing through his miraculous love. Therefore, it is for the Angie(s) of this world that I am grateful for what God has taken me through, and for the opportunities he has given me to encourage others who are hurting and feel alone.

I know suffering is not fun, and there is still a part of me that would never want to go back. But, if you asked me today if I would be willing to suffer the effects of depression all over again, I would say, "In a heartbeat!" As I look back and see what God took me through, and how he used that season of my life to help others find freedom and healing, then, "yes," I would do it all again. If I knew, in advance, what the end result would be, and how God would use the ashes of my suffering to create something beautiful, I would do it all over again. I would endure every debilitating moment if, in the end, I knew I had a future—a glorious future—formed by the grace of God to bring hope to others.

Perhaps what I am sharing is giving you a fresh perspective on your own situation. Maybe it's not. Possibly, right now, you are still chained in the bonds of depression, feeling hopeless and worried that this will never end. Or perhaps you have been set free from your bondage of depression, but you've never allowed God to use your suffering for his purposes.

Maybe you are too afraid to go back to the well. Or you don't think you can tie rags of freedom together in order to help those who have fallen. Possibly you find yourself recoiling right now. Maybe just the thought of returning to the well causes you to balk. Once you are free from that place of darkness you never want to return. Yet listen, you will not be *finally free* until you allow

> Freedom allows you to embrace your past instead of running away from it.

God to take your pain and suffering and transform it. Until you permit him to comfort others with the comfort he has given you (see 2 Corinthians 1:3-7), a part of you will remain a prisoner.

Freedom doesn't mean your circumstances have changed. Freedom means you are no longer afraid of your past. If you are free, your past no longer has a hold on you. Freedom allows you to embrace your past instead of running away from it. Freedom helps you to go back, to look at what you went through and allow those events to give someone else hope for tomorrow.

From my painful past God created Liberty in Christ Ministries. This ministry is dedicated to helping others find hope, healing, and freedom for their souls. It is a mission that declares the testimony of God's goodness and love, and was founded on the promises, "...if the Son sets you free, you will be free indeed" (John 8:36), and "It is for freedom that Christ has set us free" (Galatians 5:1). He has given me a voice, a passion, a profound awareness of his adoration, and a platform in order to share his heart and the good news of his grace and love. I have grown to love this service. Yet, this ministry was birthed from the ashes of my suffering and pain.

As I have gotten to know Jesus and handed over to him all the areas of my life, I have learned to trust God more. I have witnessed his power and love, and I have learned that he will exchange the bad for something good; he will bring hope for the future. Now, more than anything else, I want to share this love, power, grace, and mercy with the millions of people who are suffering with depression. I want them to know there is hope. In Christ, there is a way out of that well.

Through my experiences, I have learned a great deal and overcome much. This is not to say that I have it all figured out, but what my experiences have shown me is the truth behind what the speaker shared that day at the MOPS meeting. Everyone goes through life and experiences terrible heartache, lack of purpose, disappointment and disillusionment, even depression. Life will disappoint us and throw us a few curve balls. But, in the heart of her message, there was an answer to all the heartache and troubles of this world. *The only pure joy is in Jesus.*

Prior to Jesus, I didn't understand what it meant to have pure joy. I am convinced that most of the anguish I suffered in life was not because of what happened to me, but how I reacted to it. I wasted too much time worrying about life, what I had, what I didn't have. These attitudes only left me frustrated, dissatisfied, and unhappy. I bought into false expectations and mentalities. I expected other people and things to fill the void in my soul. I lost hope because what I put my confidence in was nothing but an illusion. No more!

I no longer want to put my life in the hands of empty promises, in the things that only deliver misery. I want joy—pure joy!

> Pure joy is a condition of the heart, a frame of mind that will lift up your spirits even when everything around you is falling apart.

Pure joy is not fleeting. Pure joy is not a feeling, because joy is not necessarily overwhelming feelings of gladness. You don't have to *feel* happy to have joy. It is even possible to have joy when life is unpleasant, even unfair. Pure joy is a condition of the heart, a frame of mind that will lift up your spirits even when everything around you is falling apart.

My greatest joy doesn't come when everything in life is perfect. My greatest joy comes when I am focused on Jesus and his personal love for me. The days when I take my eyes off my problems and make Jesus the center of my life, those are the days I walk with the awareness that no matter what happens in life, good or bad, he is my support and constant source of peace and joy. Now, those are the days I am *finally free*!

Share Your Story

It has been my privilege to take this journey toward freedom with you. Thank you for giving me the opportunity to share my testimony of God's healing power and love. It has been my constant prayer, as you read my story, that it has given you a fresh awareness of hope.

If God has touched your life through the pages of this book, or if you invited Jesus to come into your life as your personal Savior, I would love to hear about it. Please email me at patty@LibertyinChrist.net.

Tell me:

What chains God has broken for you?

How has God renewed your heart and revealed his love?

How has God taken you from the pit of darkness and devastation, and brought you into his light?

How has God taught you to tie rags of freedom together in order to help others?

Share anything you would like about God's love and grace. Go ahead, share your story. Start with me, and then share with others God places in your life. There is always a plan and purpose to everything we go through in life. I pray one day, you will know the fullness of God's perfect plan for your life, too.

Special Addition:

When Someone You Love is in the Well

Knowing Both Sides of the Well

In the process of writing this book, I was approached by many people who have a friend or loved one trapped in the well of depression. They are looking for answers because they don't know how to manage depression or help the one they love. I understand their desperate desire to help. I know what it is to be trapped, and I know what it is to stand on the outside of the well looking in while someone you love struggles. Both circumstances can present feelings of helplessness and hopelessness.

Nearly seven years after my bout with depression, my husband fell into the well himself. There were warning signs that his world was about to cave in. But, like he had done with me, he ignored those symptoms, hoping everything would get better. It didn't. I recognized something was wrong. And when the warning signs intensified, I must admit, at first, I felt frightened. I had been sharing my testimony publicly for some time. It's one thing to talk about my story, to point to Jesus and encourage people in their struggles, but it's another to be living with a depressed member of the family. Once my husband was clinically diagnosed, I quickly moved beyond my fear of facing that deep well again. From then on, I stood by him and we walked that journey together every step of the way.

Unlike me, my husband did end up being hospitalized. He immediately went under the care of doctors who prescribed medication. For four months the treatment helped with the symptoms, but the pills were not making him well. Fearful he would become dependent on the drugs, my husband, without the doctor's consent, decided to take himself off of his prescriptions. This decision caused his condition to worsen. For the next three months his body went through withdrawal. It was a roller coaster ride of emotional highs and lows that, at times, sent his life spinning wildly out of control.

As stated in the introduction, I am not advocating drugs as a way to find release from depression, nor am I telling you not to take medication or seek medical advice. These are personal decisions. Some forms of depression may require medication. And although medication and drugs are used to relieve symptoms of depression, they *will not cure* the depression. My purpose in sharing my husband's experience with medication is to inform you of a potential risk.

If your decision is to place your loved one on medication under a doctor's care, please stay in close contact with the doctor. Please allow your doctor to instruct you before coming off any medication. The effects of abruptly stopping medication isn't pretty, and can be dangerous.

Once the medication was completely out of his system, my husband did begin to improve emotionally and physically. In time, with therapy, lots of love, encouragement and careful attention he did begin to move forward.

As my husband gradually progressed, I had to be consistent in my role as a care-giver. I had to be a good listener. I couldn't brush the depression off, or only offer a few kind words of encouragement. That wouldn't help him. I also knew I couldn't save my husband. His release from depression wasn't in my hands, so I never tried to take on any heroics. My primary role was to be there when he needed me.

During his hospital stay, I was there for every possible hour of visitation. I listened, smiled when he talked, and held him while he cried. I witnessed every rant and tirade. After he was released, we went for long walks in the park in order to get him out of the house. For a change of pace we took our family on a mini-vacation, thinking the change of scenery would help—it did.

During this dark time, I knew the importance of staying focused on Jesus. Since I clung to him as my sole source of support, I never lost hope. I believed Jesus could free my husband if he would open his heart and respond to him. This resolve gave me the strength to encourage my husband, to be optimistic, and reassure him that God loved him and longed to give him a way out.

It took almost a year for my husband to be set free from depression. He didn't experience the instant deliverance I had, but God healed him nonetheless. Trusting God is critical. As I said earlier, God is sovereign. The way he chooses to heal is completely in his hands. My freedom from depression came when I came to the end of myself and admitted my need for God. But through my husband's experiences, he learned to trust God as he surrendered more and more of his life one day at a time. Today, he knows Jesus as both his Savior and his healer.

On this journey toward emotional freedom with your loved one, I would like to offer you some practical tips, a list of do's and don'ts that worked for me when handling someone with depression. They may not work for everyone, but hopefully these tips will offer you support and give you a more effective approach. I am not a doctor. I cannot offer you professional advice. I can only tell you what I learned, based on personal depression experience, and what I learned during my husband's struggle.

- **Don't assume your loved one will be fine:** My husband didn't understand, so he thought I would be fine or that I would somehow just "get over it."

- **Keep yourself encouraged:** Depression is overwhelming for everyone involved. Caregivers need to stay emotionally healthy. It is vital to keep your focus on Jesus. Join a support group or Bible study.

- **Be a good listener:** Be patient, listen attentively and when responding don't judge or criticize how the person feels.

- **Be transparent:** Do not say you understand if you've never struggled with depression. Do share about a time when you struggled emotionally. Your transparency can help. Don't expect or force a response. Becoming vulnerable might make him/her feel weak. It is risky to lay the soul bare and exposed. Be patient. Affirm that you are there for them and when he/she chooses to talk, you will be eager to listen.

- **Don't ask generalized questions:** "How are you feeling?" "Is everything okay?" These questions are too vague and only lead to vague responses. Ask open-ended questions that will require more than a "yes" or "no" answer.

- **Don't panic if your loved one starts talking about suicide:** Don't become upset or frightened. Just because a person talks about taking their life, doesn't automatically mean they will. You will not put them in danger by listening. Instead, you could be protecting your loved one by allowing that person to express feelings. Avoid engaging in conversations centered on ways to commit suicide. Depressed people may be feeling suicidal, but may have no idea how to go about it. Pay attention to the person's emotional state and try your best to redirect any discussion about specific methods of suicide to a more positive topic.

- **Get him/her out of the house:** Depressed people are prone to hide. They don't want to be around others. They will need some help and encouragement to get beyond this place of isolation. Regularly invite your loved one to join you for a walk, dinner out, or someplace fun. Tap into what he/she loved to do before the depression symptoms appeared.

- **Smile:** A happy face, bright attitude and cheerful actions may help to lift a downcast spirit.

- **Watch for changes in behavior:** Look for changes in sleep patterns, loss of appetite, or turning to drugs or alcohol. Look for any changes that are out of the ordinary for this person.

- **Don't take it personally:** Your loved one may, at times, push you away. This is no reflection on you or the relationship. It's a symptom of the illness. Be understanding. Don't let unkind responses discourage you or dismantle the relationship. This behavior stems from an involuntary and irrational reaction. It's not a personal attack.

- **Hold onto faith:** Above all, don't lose hope. Your loved one is encouraged best when those around him/her remain hopeful. Assure him/her often of God's love. Read Scripture and play Christian music.

To help you and your loved one find encouragement, I have put together a list of Scripture verses on the next page. These *Words of Hope* are meant to support and uplift you both during this time.

Words of Hope

"Why so downcast, O my soul? Why so disturbed within me? Put your hope in God, for I will yet praise Him, my Savior and my God" (Psalm 42:5).

"In this world you will have trouble. But take heart! I have overcome the world" (John 16:33).

"Cast all your anxiety upon him because he cares for you" (1 Peter 5:7).

"Come to me, all you who are weary and burdened, and I will give you rest. Take my yoke upon you and learn from me, for I am gentle and humble in heart, and you will find rest for your souls" (Matthew 11:28-29).

"So do not fear. For I am with you; do not be dismayed, for I your God. I will strengthen you and help you; I will uphold you with my righteous right hand" (Isaiah 41:10).

"Weeping may remain for a night, but rejoicing comes in the morning" (Psalm 30:5b).

"I will build you up again, and you will be rebuilt.... Again you will take up your tambourines and go out to dance with the joyful" (Jeremiah 31:4).

"…it is for freedom that Christ has set us free" (Galatians 5:1).

"So if the Son sets you free, you will be free indeed" (John 8:36).

"Those who hope in the LORD will renew their strength" (Isaiah 40:31).

"The LORD is close to the brokenhearted and saves those who are crushed in spirit" (Psalm 34:18).

"Some sat in darkness and the deepest gloom, prisoners suffering in iron chains…. Then they cried to the LORD in their troubles, and he saved them from their distress. He brought them out of darkness and the deepest gloom and broke away their chains" (Psalm 107:10;13-14).

"Praise the LORD, O my soul, and forget not all his benefits—who forgives all your sins and heals all your diseases, who redeems your life from the pit and crowns you with love and compassion" (Psalm 103:2-4).

"The people walking in darkness have seen a great light; on those living in the land of the shadow of death a light has dawned" (Isaiah 9:2).

Hope for the Future

"For I know the plans I have for you,' declares the LORD, 'plans to prosper you and not to harm you, plans to give you a hope and a future" (Jeremiah 29:11).

"Trust in the LORD with all your heart and lean not on your own understanding; in all your ways acknowledge Him, and he will make your paths straight" (Proverbs 3:5-6).

"...the LORD has anointed me to preach good news to the poor. He has sent me to bind up the brokenhearted, to proclaim freedom for the captives and release from darkness for the prisoners" (Isaiah 61:1).

"The ransomed of the LORD will return. They will enter Zion with singing; everlasting joy will crown their heads. Gladness and joy will overtake them, and sorrow and sighing will flee away" (Isaiah 51:11).

"Praise...the Father of compassion and the God of all comfort, who comforts us in all our troubles, so that we can comfort those in any trouble with the comfort we ourselves have received from God" (2 Corinthians 1:3-4).

Endnotes

Introduction

[i] Cymbalta:
http://cymbalta.com/depression/understandingdepression.jsp?WT.seg_1
=MDD&DCSext.ag=GeneralResearch&WT.mc_id=CymMDDA65580001&
WT.srch=1

[ii] Uplift Program:
http://www.upliftprogram.com/depression_stats.html#statistics
Bob Murray, PHD. Alicia Fortinberry, MS

Chapter Two

[iii] Barney
A six-foot purple dinosaur, Barney stars in the children's TV show *Barney and Friends*. The character got his start in 1987 in direct-sale videos created by Dallas teacher Sheryl Leach.
"Barney & Friends" began airing on television in 1992.
To learn more go to:
http://wiki.answers.com/Q/What_is_the_year_Barney_the_dinosaur_came_on_TV#ixzz18JpP7P3j

Chapter Eight

[iv] *Damaged Goods: Learning to Dream Again*, Charlotte Hunt, (Dream Madly Publishers: 2010)
To learn more, go to: http://www.charlottehunt.com/
(used with author's permission)

[v] *A Scarlet Cord of Hope: My Journey through Guilt, Shame, and Fear to Hope*, Sheryl Griffin, (Westview Publishers, Inc., Nashville, TN: 2010)
To learn more, go to: http://www.sherylgriffin.com/
(used with author's permission)

Acknowlededgments

A very special thank you to Charlotte Hunt, Sheryl Griffin, Teresa Rose, Laurence Tumpag and the other precious souls who were willing to contribute to this book by sharing their testimonies of hardship and faith. May God bless you richly for your continued trust in him.

I want to extend a word of thanks to all the people who have made a difference in my life. Terry Delong, Sue Jacox, Miriam Nodzo, Vivian Good and David Noel, you are my mentors, the ones who have stood beside me through my personal journey, continually cheering me on toward the goal, helping me remain focused on what is most important.

I want to thank my husband and family for their unwavering support. It's a scary thing to record your life on paper; it's even scarier to publish your life for others to read. This book was never meant to hurt those I love, air dirty laundry, or disparage anyone's character. I spoke with my husband and parents prior to publishing this book, and all three have encouraged me to share my story. In many ways, sharing this book with my family brought us closer together and gave us a greater level of appreciation and respect for each other. I love my family dearly, and could not have openly shared some of the aspects of this book without their consent.

I want to thank my children for loving me unconditionally. They were very young at the time of the depression; yet, the love they showed during that time was immeasurable and priceless. At times, it was the only thing that pulled me through some of those dark days. My children are amazing. I am proud of them; and, in spite of that terrible time, they have grown into wonderful teenagers and young adults.

I especially want to acknowledge my oldest daughter. While I was writing this book, we had an opportunity to talk about her childhood and what happened during the depression. To my amazement, she told me she only remembered two incidents. Unlike the first time I asked her to forgive me, she smiled warmly and hugged me as if to say that my apology was unnecessary. But it was necessary—not only for her, but for me. As we hugged, it reminded me of the incomparable joy of forgiveness and love.

Thank you to all the wonderful women who graciously took the time to review the manuscript and offer encouragement, advise and recommendations. Your thoughts on this project were greatly appreciated. I couldn't have done this project without your support.

Diane Mendez, once again, you have come through for me. Your expertise and skills in the publishing arena are invaluable. You're the best!

Finally, I want to acknowledge all the dear souls who approached me during this venture to share their hearts and hurts, struggles and pain. It was your stories that kept me on track to finish this book. I must admit, in moments of weakness, I wondered if what I was doing would make a difference in the lives of others. Many people are searching for answers; and, at times, I worried if my story would be enough. But, as I listened to one of your stories, I would once again be reminded of the reason why I was writing this book. And, as I shared my story with you in return, I could see hope form in your eyes and would remember that my story points to Jesus. Jesus is enough. Jesus is the answer we all seek to find.

Therefore, to my loving Savior and Lord, thank you for saving me. Thank you for being there in my darkest hour. Thank you for reaching into my well of depression, pulling me out and placing my life on the solid ground of your love. You, and you alone, broke the bonds of my depression without drugs. You are what I have searched for all my life—the answer to all my quests. You have filled my life with direction and purpose. You are my constant hope for today and tomorrow. You are the reason I have joy.

Liberty in Christ Ministries

Finding Freedom for the Soul

To learn more about the ministry God created through my darkness, please visit: www.LibertyinChrist.net

If you are still suffering with depression, please feel free to email me. I'd love to stand with you in prayer. Or if you have a story of hope, and of the power of God's healing and love, I would love to hear your testimony. Please contact me at patty@LibertyinChrist.net

About the Author

Patty Mason is an award-winning author, speaker, and the founder of Liberty in Christ Ministries. She has been teaching, mentoring and inspiring women of all ages through her writings and her talks. Patty has reached audiences all over the world through Sisters on Assignment, ChristianTV, Salem Communications Network Channel Light Source, and as a co-host on WLGT Blog Radio Live.

"I understand how the hurts of a painful past can hinder you and keep you from receiving the love of God with your whole heart. My passion and purpose is to help you find hope, healing and freedom for your soul, by helping you experience the ardent love of Jesus. What do you need to be set free from? What is consuming your life, holding you captive and not allowing you to live the abundant life that Jesus promised? Let go of all the garbage and baggage that is weighing you down, learn how to spread your wings and fly to new heights of love."

If you would like to invite Patty to come and share at your next event or group meeting, please feel free to email her at patty@LibertyinChrist.net

Other Books by this Author

TRANSFORMED BY DESIRE:
A Journey of Awakening to Life and Love

What do you yearn for? What are the longings that you ache to fill? What have you kept buried within your soul that needs to be uncovered? The journey of a lifetime begins with desire, desire that will stir your heart and awaken your soul, desire that will thrust your life into new levels of meaning and purpose. God longs for you to open your heart and mind. To ask—seek—knock, to take a journey of longing. God has implanted desires within you, let them come alive with new life and love. Dare to dream; dare to embrace the truest desires of your heart. Dare to answer the question: *What are the desires of my heart?*

Available to Order!
Only $14.99, plus shipping
To order go to www.LibertyinChrist.net

TRANSFORMED BY DESIRE Bible Study:
A Journey of Awakening to Life and Love

Explore the passions of Christ's heart with award-winning author and speaker Patty Mason. Catch Patty's passion and infectious enthusiasm as she stirs your heart to pursue greater levels of intimacy with Jesus. By tapping into the truest desires of your heart you will...

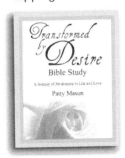

- Discover God's desires for you
- Receive joy that never ends
- Embrace God's passionate heart toward you
- Understand your worth in His eyes
- Learn to value yourself

The Journey of a Lifetime Begins with Desire
This in-depth Bible study is perfect for personal quiet times, book clubs, or group study.

Available to Order!
Only $16.99, plus shipping
To order go to www.LibertyinChrist.net

Bible Study comes with a free Leader's Guide eBook
and complete video series